THE
Hidden
Disorder

THE
Hidden Disorder

A Clinician's Guide
to Attention Deficit
Hyperactivity
Disorder in
Adults

Robert J. Resnick, PhD

American Psychological Association
Washington, DC

First Printing June 2000
Second Printing January 2004

Published by
American Psychological Association
750 First Street, NE
Washington, DC 20002

Copies may be ordered from
APA Order Department
P.O. Box 92984
Washington, DC 20090-2984

In the U.K., Europe, Africa, and the Middle East, copies may be ordered from
American Psychological Association
3 Henrietta Street
Covent Garden, London
WC2E 8LU England

Typeset in Meridien by EPS Group Inc., Easton, MD

Printer: Automated Graphics Systems, White Plains, MD
Cover Designer: Naylor Design, Washington, DC
Technical/Production Editor: Jennifer Powers

The opinions and statements published are the responsibility of the authors, and such opinions and statements do not necessarily represent the policies of the APA.

Library of Congress Cataloging-in-Publication Data

Resnick, Robert J.
    The hidden disorder : a clinician's guide to attention deficit hyperactivity disorder in adults / Robert J. Resnick.
        p.   cm.
    Includes bibliographical references and index.
    ISBN 1-55798-724-6 (alk. paper)
        1. Attention-deficit disorder in adults.   2. Attention-deficit disordered adults.
    3. Attention-deficit hyperactivity disorder.   I. Title.
        [DNLM: 1. Attention Deficit Disorder with Hyperactivity—diagnosis—Adult.
    2. Attention Deficit Disorder with Hyperactivity—therapy—Adult.
    WL 354 R467h 2000]
    RC394 A85 R49 2000
    616.85'89—dc21
                                                                        00-032283

British Library Cataloguing-in-Publication Data
A CIP record is available from the British Library

Printed in the United States of America

To my wife Fran, who always said I should write a book.

To our daughters Danielle and Jolene, who said that they would read the book (or at least skim it), and to our son Steven, who taught me more about attention deficit disorders than I ever wanted to know.

And last, to Charlene Price Resnick, Steven's wife, who not only loves and accepts him for what he is, but is also helping him become more than he was.

Contents

9

Preface

You have to deal with the fact that your life is your life.
—Alex Haley

am a child and health psychologist by training and experience. Because of my son's problems with attention and concentration, followed by inaccurate or erroneous diagnoses and treatments, I became more and more interested in attention deficits. Quite by accident of geography and location, I became involved with the National Institute of Mental Health field trials for the new nomenclature and diagnostic criteria used in the *Diagnostic and Statistical Manual of Mental Disorders* (*DSM-III*; American Psychiatric Association, 1980). This was the edition that introduced us to "Attention Deficit Disorder," with and without hyperactivity with accompanying evaluative criteria. Language and criteria were modified through the *DSM-III-R* in 1987 and again in 1994 in the *DSM-IV* to the language used today: "Attention Deficit/Hyperactivity Disorder" (ADHD) with the modifiers of Predominantly Inattentive Type, Predominantly Impulsive–Hyperactive Type, and Combined Type.

On July 1, 1984, as Professor and Chair of the Division of Clinical Psychology at the Medical College of Virginia, Health Sciences Center, Virginia Commonwealth University, I started the Attention Deficits Disorders Clinic. I directed that program until June 30, 1996, having left the university on a faculty early retirement program. From the program's beginning, one parent or the other, sometimes both, had clear recollections of having the same or similar ADHD problems as did their children. "The apple doesn't fall far from the tree" was said more times than I can recall. These parents often commented in passing that, in some ways, they were still troubled by inattention, disorganization, and forgetfulness. On occasion parents would ask if everybody "outgrows"

ADHD. With greater public awareness of ADHD, parents began to understand that most children with attention deficits do not outgrow the disorder. More parents began asking about their own problems with attention and asked whether the clinic could evaluate them.

Initially, the clinic would not, as we feared being overwhelmed with adults at the expense of the children. But the demand increased, and the decision was made to start a parallel, but unofficial, program for adults. In thinking back, in a way we were clearly forced into this decision, as adults would ask where they could go for evaluation and possible treatment. Very few practitioners, if any, were adequately grounded in the adult presentation of this disorder. We, at least, could extrapolate from our child work experience of this disorder and try it with adults.

Adult ADHD is clearly a hidden disorder. Although there are many adults who know that they have attention problems, there are even more who do not know. For the many who are being treated appropriately, there are likely many more whose attention problems and their consequences are not being addressed. Shortly after we began the adult program, it became clear that many more practitioners were needed who were knowledgeable in the diagnosis and treatment of adult attention deficit disorders.

This book is written for the busy clinician who needs a practical guide in the diagnosis and treatment of adult attention deficit disorders. It is relatively brief and to the point. I have purposefully not overloaded the text with citations and book references. My intention is to provide the reader with a framework, building on existing skills, to identify and treat ADHD in adults. At the end of the book, however, there are references and resources for those who wish more detailed information in a given content area and for practitioners to use in their work.

References

American Psychiatric Association. (1980). *Diagnostic and statistical manual of mental disorders* (3rd ed.). Washington, DC: Author.

American Psychiatric Association. (1987). *Diagnostic and statistical manual of mental disorders* (3rd ed., rev.). Washington, DC: Author.

American Psychiatric Association. (1994). *Diagnostic and statistical manual of mental disorders* (4th ed.). Washington, DC: Author.

Cook, J. (1997). *The book of positive quotations.* Minneapolis, MN: Fairview Press.

Acknowledgments

I t was Gary VandenBos, PhD, Executive Director, APA Communications, who first approached me about writing this book. In fact he kept "approaching me" for almost two years before he finally wore me down. Now that I have finished the book I know that I am grateful to Gary.

Second, I am also very grateful to Jessica Sins who, in addition to being a full-time student and part-time receptionist, found the time to transcribe the manuscript. Even more startling was her unerring ability to read my edits. Jessica joins an elite list that can be enumerated on the fingers of one hand who are able to read my handwriting.

So, too, am I appreciative to my friends and colleagues at Dominion Behavioral Healthcare who offered suggestions and comments—Yael Buchsbaum, PhD; Steven Butnick, PhD; Julia Frishtick, LCSW; Diane Hensley, LCSW; and Gail Quick, PhD. Thanks and kudos also go to Meredith W. Green, PhD, a senior psychologist in general practice; "Mac" Horton, PhD, a psychologist who has worked with and has researched attention deficit hyperactivity disorder (ADHD); and Steven J. Resnick, a lifelong member of the "ADHD club," for their very helpful suggestions about the manuscript. To Dr. Kathy Nadeau and Dr. Michael Linden, who read and commented on the manuscript, I am most indebted.

A word of thanks to Judy A. Nemes, APA Development Editor; Chris Davis, APA Supervisor, Technical Editing and Design; and Jennifer Powers, APA Technical/Production Editor, for their efficiency and collaborative efforts.

And last, thanks go to all of the adults with ADHD who have shared their sadness, frustrations, goals, and ambitions. They have all contributed to my understanding and knowledge. They are the living truth; they all don't outgrow it!

THE
Hidden
Disorder

"Fidgety Phil" to *DSM-IV*: 135 Years of Hyperactivity

1

In times like these, it helps to recall that there have always been times like these.

—Paul Harvey

German physician Heinrich Hoffman (1865) wrote a nursery rhyme that described a restless, fidgety, and overactive child during a family meal:

> Philipp, stop acting like a worm
> The table is no place to squirm . . .
> But Philipp will not take advice,
> He'll have his way at any price.
> He turns, and churns, he wiggles and jiggles,
> Here and there on the chair.

This may be the first documented case of attention deficit hyperactivity disorder (ADHD), although retrospectively, many famous individuals in history have been identified with similar behavior—Alexander the Great, Genghis Khan, and Thomas Alva Edison to name but a few. Earlier, the English physician Alexander Crichton (1798) had a chapter "On Attention and Its Diseases" in the textbook *An Inquiry Into the Nature and Origin of Mental Derangement*. However, it was not until the 20th century that George F. Still (1902) described certain behaviors in children that were most closely related to ADHD. The anomaly was known then as "Still's disease," even though this behavioral condition was called a "brain damage syndrome." Still postulated that the major problem of these children was "defective moral control," because they were seen as exhibiting poor self-control, overactivity, fidgetiness, immaturity, ag-

Originally published in *The School Psychologist*, Vol. 2, p. 4. Copyright 1993 by the Division of School Psychology of the American Psychological Association. Adapted with permission.

gressiveness, defiance, cruelty, and dishonesty, along with lying and stealing. He described children with these behaviors as vicious, shameless, sexually immoral, and wanton.

The interest in attention deficit in the United States was heightened by an outbreak of Van Economo's encephalitis in 1917–1918. The pandemic caused many postdisease behavior disorders marked by hyperactivity, coordination deficits, learning disabilities, impulsivity, and aggressive behavior (Kessler, 1980). These observations were consistent with what Still had reported earlier, and an early link between brain damage or central nervous system dysfunction and hyperactivity was made. Thus, the connection of encephalitis to these ADHD-like behaviors lent credence to the belief that these children had specific nervous system damage, and the theory of brain damage syndrome was born. A few years later, "organically driven" was used to describe these children, with some belief that the problem lay in brain stem damage. This damage in turn was thought to cause general overactivity and clumsiness, as well as behavioral disinhibition. Early researchers in the area of hyperactivity thought that, although being organically driven was a result of prenatal or birth injury or disease, there also might be a genetic disposition to these symptoms. The symptoms themselves were seen as a "constitutional variant." It was, in fact, in the early 1930s that the first suggestion of a genetic predisposition toward hyperactivity was made by D. L. Pauls (1991), an observation that was confirmed many years later.

An important event in the history of ADHD occurred in 1937 at the Emma Pendleton Bradley Home in Rhode Island. For almost four decades this facility undertook a series of studies using Benzedrine (dextroamphetamine sulfate) to treat children with an "organic brain syndrome" (Bradley, 1937; Bradley & Bowen, 1940; Molitch & Eccles, 1937). This medication seemed to be effective in reducing disruptive behavior and improving school performance in hospitalized children with behavior disorders. During those years these children were given diagnoses such as "hyper-kinetic impulse disorder," "developmental hyperactivity," "hyperactive child syndrome," "hyper-kinetic child syndrome," and "restless syndrome." Such diagnoses continued to foster the belief that most of these children's behaviors were the sequelae of organic damage.

Shortly after the end of World War II, the term "minimal brain dysfunction" began finding its way into the literature on children with behavior disorders (see Strauss & Lehtinen, 1947). Available data showed that children with brain damage did not behave in ways similar to children with no demonstrable brain damage, although they had many of the symptoms earlier attributed to children with such deficits.

Evolution of ADHD in the DSM Criteria

DSM AND DSM-II

With the publication of the *Diagnostic and Statistical Manual of Mental Disorders* (*DSM;* American Psychiatric Association, 1952), the diagnosis was conceptualized as "Minimal Brain Damage" or "Hyperkinetic Syndrome." The *DSM-II* (American Psychiatric Association, 1968) introduced "Hyperkinetic Reaction of Childhood and Adolescence." However, by the late 1950s and early 1960s, articles in the professional literature were criticizing the concept that minimal brain damage exhibited only behavioral signs without commensurate neurological deficits.

In 1963, when the 91st Congress passed the Developmental Disabilities Assistance and Bill of Rights Act (P. L. 88–164), scholarly interest in minimal brain damage and brain dysfunction had moved to the level of public policy, as taxpayers' dollars became available for children who had learning disabilities. In that same year, the Oxford International Study Group in Child Neurology concluded that minimal brain damage should be discarded and replaced by "minimal brain dysfunction," primarily because brain damage should never be inferred from behavioral signs alone. The group also concluded that children with minimal brain dysfunction comprised a heterogeneous group with several possible syndromes or clusters. Interestingly, in 1963, when the Easter Seal Foundation sponsored a conference with the U.S. Health Services' Division of Chronic Diseases, the conference also adopted the term "minimal brain dysfunction." It then listed 99 symptoms and signs exhibited by children who were so diagnosed. There was still no consensus on patient presentation.

DSM-III

In the early 1970s, the American Psychiatric Association created study groups to redefine psychiatric diagnoses in preparation for the release of the *DSM-III* (1980). In 1978–1979, the National Institute of Health sponsored a field trial for the new manual. The diagnostic categories field tested were "Attention Deficit Disorder (ADD) with Hyperactivity," "ADD without Hyperactivity," and "ADD residual type in adulthood." This was the first professional acknowledgment, although there was minimal research data at the time, to suggest that not everyone "outgrew" their attention deficit disorder (and that attention deficits can exist without hyperactivity). Although this was a significant step forward, clinicians were concerned that ADD residual type in adulthood implied that hyperactivity was not a part of the adult presentation, but such implications were in error. It was clear that adults were demonstrating that the expression of the hyperactivity by adulthood often changes into more age-acceptable and tolerated behaviors, such as finger thumping, ankle wiggling, key chain rattling, or simply a subjective sense of heightened tension when the individual was required to remain seated for an extended period of time. Hyperactivity, as a symptom, is not uniformly absent in all adult presentations of ADD. These changes from *DSM-II* to *DSM-III* were important because the latter emphasized inattention and distractibility in the presence or absence of hyperactivity. Practicing clinicians had, for years, seen that children, adolescents, and adults can present grave problems with inattention and distractibility without demonstrating significant evidence of a hyperactive component.

DSM-III-R

The *DSM-III-R* (American Psychiatric Association, 1987) reasserted the primacy of hyperactivity and impulsivity as the core behavioral symptoms within attention disorders. The work group on disruptive disorders concluded, from their thorough review of then-available research, that the symptoms of overactivity and impulsivity were related because of the nondiscriminating capacity of the symptoms when making a diagnosis. That is, there was little evidence to support the belief that impulsivity and hyperactivity were different dimensions, and there was little evidence that these two behaviors could be measured as separate symptoms. Thus, the work group opted to make attention deficits a unitary concept with a single list of 13 diagnostic criteria enumerated with any 8 endorsements sufficient to an ADHD diagnosis.

I have seen many children and adults who are impulsive but who exhibit little or no hyperactivity. From speaking with colleagues, my experience is not the exception. The diagnostic criteria used in the *DSM-III-R* were so broad that many nonhyperactive children who would have been diagnosed with ADD without hyperactivity were now considered hyperactive. A new category, "Undifferentiated Attention Deficit Disorder," confused matters even more. ADHD was a diagnosis found in the category "Disruptive Disorders" with diagnostic criteria, whereas Undifferentiated ADD was in the category "Other Disorders" with no diagnostic criteria. The *DSM-III-R* was not instructive as to where one would place a child with attention deficits without hyperactivity or where one should place the residual type or adult attention deficits.

The decision to separate the two disorders was seen, at least in part, as a political solution to internal disagreements. Where the *DSM-III* had three symptom lists (impulsivity, inattention, and hyperactivity) and permitted the diagnosis of ADD without hyperactivity, the *DSM-III-R* did not permit the diagnosis. Thus, whereas the *DSM-III* generally was more restrictive in its criteria, the *DSM-III-R* became broad and more incorporative and, consequently, tended to be overly inclusive and diagnostic.

DSM-IV

In 1994, the *DSM-IV* superseded the *DSM-III-R*. It labeled all attention deficits as "hyperactive." There is "ADHD primarily inattentive type" and "ADHD primarily hyperactive–impulsive type." In this paradigm, it is as if when one says "hyperactive" once one does not really mean it, but if one says it twice one really does. In addition, there are categories of "ADHD Combined Types" showing both inattentiveness as well as hyperactivity–impulsivity and "ADHD Not Otherwise Specified" for those who exhibit symptoms of ADHD but who do not meet the full criteria. This is highly confusing to patients with ADHD, their families, and their employers alike.

The *DSM-IV* criteria are reportedly consistent among all ages and, therefore, no separate criteria for adults are listed. This poses problems, as the existing criteria are more targeted for school-age children. Also, some of the criteria do not translate well into adult behavior, such as "often on the go," "often acts like driven by motor," or "often has difficulty sustaining attention in tasks or play activities."

Implications and Language

Adult-based norms for *DSM-IV* criteria are greatly needed. One hopes that adult-based criteria will be part of the *DSM-V*. In the meantime, clinicians, in applying some of the *DSM-IV* criteria, will need to modify them for an adult environment. For example, problems in school could be translated into problems on the job. Are we diagnosing more adults with ADHD? Absolutely. Have the numbers increased over time? That is hard to tell. For generations it was thought that everyone always outgrew ADHD. Now it is known that many individuals continue to have significant difficulties into adulthood. More recently, practitioners are increasingly noting adults who exhibit debilitating inattention but are not hyperactive.

Although the vast majority of research and writing on ADHD is generated in the United States, attention deficits occur all over the world. The World Health Organization (WHO) recognized the disorder, and hyperkinetic and conduct disorder are listed in the *International Classification of Diseases (ICD-10;* WHO, 1992). Such internationality of ADHD symptoms makes it imperative that standard and consistent nomenclature, terminology, and diagnostic criteria be developed.

For the purposes of this book I refer to all attention deficit disorders as ADHD. When it is appropriate to specifically discuss the hyperactive impulsive, inattentive, or combined types, I will add the additional qualifiers.

References and Resources

American Psychiatric Association. (1952). *Diagnostic and statistical manual of mental disorders.* Washington, DC: Author.

American Psychiatric Association. (1968). *Diagnostic and statistical manual of mental disorders* (2nd ed.). Washington, DC: Author.

American Psychiatric Association. (1980). *Diagnostic and statistical manual of mental disorders* (3rd ed.). Washington, DC: Author.

American Psychiatric Association. (1987). *Diagnostic and statistical manual of mental disorders* (3rd ed., rev.). Washington, DC: Author.

American Psychiatric Association. (1994). *Diagnostic and statistical manual of mental disorders* (4th ed.). Washington, DC: Author.

Barkley, R. A. (1998). *Attention-deficit-hyperactivity disorder: A handbook for diagnosis and treatment* (2nd ed.). New York: Guilford Press.

Bradley, W. (1937). The behavior of children receiving benzedrine. *American Journal of Psychiatry, 94,* 577–585.

Bradley, W., & Bowen, C. (1940). School performance of children receiving amphetamine (benzedrine) sulfate. *American Journal of Orthopsychiatry, 10,* 782–788.

Cook, J. (1997). *The book of positive quotations.* Minneapolis, MN: Fairview Press.

Crichton, A. (1798). On attention and its diseases. In T. Cadell, Jr. & W. Davies (Eds.), *An inquiry into the nature and origin of mental derangement* (Vol. 1, pp. 254–290). London: The Strand.

Developmental Disabilities Assistance and Bill of Rights Act, Pub. L. 88-164, 77 Stat. 282 (1963).

Hoffman, H. (1865). Die Geschichte vom Zappel-Philipp. In *Der Struwwelpeter.* Germany: Pestalozzi-Verlag.

Kessler, J. W. (1980). History of minimal brain dysfunction. In H. Rie & E. Rie (Eds.), *Handbook of minimal brain dysfunctions: A critical review* (pp. 18–52). New York: Wiley.

Molitch, M., & Eccles, A. K. (1937). Effect of benzedrine sulphate on intelligence scores of children. *American Journal of Psychiatry, 94,* 587–590.

Pauls, D. L. (1991). Genetic factor and the expression of attention/deficit-hyperactivity disorder. *Journal of Child and Adolescent Psychopharmacology, 1,* 353–360.

Resnick, R. J. (1993). From Fidgety Phil to *DSM-IV*: 125 years of hyperactivity. *School Psychologist, 2,* 4.

Still, G. F. (1902). Some abnormal psychical conditions in children. *Lancet, 1,* 1008–1012, 1077–1082, 1163–1168.

Strauss, A. A., & Lehtinen, L. E. (1947). *Psychopathology and education of the brain-injured child.* New York: Grune & Stratton.

Wender, P. (1971). *Minimal brain dysfunction.* New York: Wiley.

World Health Organization. (1992). *International classification of diseases* (10th ed.). Geneva, Switzerland: Author.

ADHD Through the Life Span

2

The art of living lies less in eliminating our troubles than by growing with them.

—Bernard M. Baruch

Adults who present in the therapist's office with ADHD symptoms have been experiencing these symptoms all of their lives. This chapter discusses the development of ADHD from childhood through adulthood: the prevalence of the disease; its etiology; diversity issues that relate to ADHD, such as ethnicity, gender, and socioeconomic status (SES); and ADHD as manifested in adulthood. Four core symptoms of ADHD form the basis for understanding how the individual with ADHD functions.

Prevalence

The prevalence of ADD is estimated at 3% to 5% of school-age children in the United States (American Psychiatric Association, 1994; Barkley, 1998). Some estimates place the number as high as 20%. The lower estimate translates into approximately 3.5 million children. These figures do not take into account preschool, adolescent, and adult populations.

Prevalence rates vary according to the population sampled, the diagnostic criteria, and the diagnostic instruments used (Cantwell, 1996). But even when similar diagnostic criteria are used, the percentages diverge across cultures and countries, suggesting that ethnic and cultural acceptance of ADD symptoms greatly affect the threshold at which "normal" behaviors become ADD symptoms (Barkley, 1998; Gingerich, Turnock, Litfin, & Rosen, 1998). For example, two epidemiological studies using *DSM-IV* criteria were recently reported, one conducted in Tennessee (Wolraich, Hannah, Pinnock, Baumgaertel, & Brown, 1996) and the other in Germany (Baumgaertel, Wolraich, & Dietrich, 1995). The prevalence rates in the Tennessee sample were 4.7% for the primarily inattentive, 3.4% for the primarily hyperactive, and 4.4% for the combined subtypes of ADHD in the *DSM-IV.* Rates for the German sample for the same subtypes were 9.0%, 3.9%, and 4.8%, respectively.

In both clinical and epidemiological samples, ADHD is predominantly noted in males. Gender ratios of males to females vary considerably across studies, from 2:1 to 10:1 (Ross & Ross, 1982). The average ratios most often cited for U.S. children is 6:1 for clinic-referred samples (Barkley, 1998) and 3:1 for epidemiological samples (Szatmari, Offord, & Boyle, 1989). Researchers have suggested that these gender differences may be the result of a selective referral bias: Girls tend to exhibit more inattentive and cognitive problems relative to boys, who tend to have the aggressive–impulsive conduct symptomatology that leads to earlier referral (Baumgaertel et al., 1995; Cantwell, 1996; Wolraich et al., 1996). Barkley (1998) noted that the predominantly hyperactive–impulsive type seems to be almost exclusively diagnosed among younger children and is frequently the precursor to the combined-type diagnosis in later childhood.

How prevalent is ADHD in adult life? Various methodological approaches to estimating prevalence all arrive at a reliable approximation of 4%. Barkley's (1998) epidemiological study suggested 4.7%. M. Weiss, Hechtman, and Weiss (1999) concluded that assuming that two-thirds of children have residual ADHD symptoms in adulthood and if that prevalence in childhood is 3% to 6%, then 2% to 4% of people who had ADHD as children would continue to have the disorder as adults. If the *DSM-IV* estimate of the prevalence of ADHD in children is used, and one assumes that two-thirds will continue to have ADHD as they grow to adulthood, then 8% to 12% of adults would meet the diagnostic criteria. Thus, prevalence of ADHD in adulthood is estimated to be between a low of 2% and a high of 10%.

Etiology

The etiology of ADHD is complex and not completely understood. Evidence indicates that ADHD does not stem from home environment, but instead from biological causes (National Institute of Mental Health [NIMH], 1999). As new tools and techniques for studying the brain emerge, scientists have been able to test more theories about the causes of ADHD.

There appears to be general agreement that ADHD involves a neurochemical transmission problem in the brain. The prefrontal lobe of the cerebral cortex suffers from an insufficiency of the chemical transmitters dopamine and norepinephrine. These deficiencies in the neurochemical transmitting environment produce the deficits in behavioral inhibition, working memory, regulation of motivation, and motor control.

NIMH scientists demonstrated a link between a person's ability to pay continued attention and the level of activity in the brain. Using a positron emission tomography scanner, the researchers measured the level of glucose used by the areas of the brain that inhibit impulses and control attention. Glucose is the brain's main source of energy, and it is a good indicator of the brain's activity level. Important differences were found between adults who had ADHD and those who did not. In adults with ADHD, the brain areas that control attention used less glucose, indicating that this part of the brain was less active. Thus, the research indicated that a lower level of activity in some parts of the brain may cause inattention.

Several other risk factors are associated with the development of ADHD. Most of them are related to the intrauterine environment, complications at birth, or complications immediately postpartum. Virtually any medical problem that may arise during the 270 days of gestation could be a risk factor. Researchers are looking into how the brain normally develops in the fetus and examining how the brain works when the nerve cells are connected correctly or incorrectly. Scientists are tracking some factors that impede the proper connection of brain cells during fetal development, such as smoking and drug use during pregnancy, exposure to toxins, and genetics.

Heavy alcohol use during pregnancy could distort developing nerve cells in the fetus resulting in fetal alcohol syndrome (FAS). This condi-

FRANK AND ERNEST reprinted by permission of Newspaper Enterprise Association, Inc.

tion can lead to low birth weight, intellectual impairment, and physical defects. Children with FAS exhibit the same behaviors as children with ADHD (i.e., hyperactivity, inattention, and impulsivity). FAS may also contribute to the development of ADHD.

Drug use during pregnancy may also harm the normal development of brain receptors in the fetus. Some researchers believe that children exposed to environmental toxins such as lead (found in dust, soil, flaking paint, and water pipes) that disrupt brain development or brain processes may develop ADHD symptoms, but only a few cases have been found.

Low birth weight may also contribute to the development of ADHD. Similarly, a postmature or premature delivery, a breech delivery, or a delivery by cesarean section appear to be risk factors. Any problem immediately postpartum, such as anoxia or jaundice, are also risk factors, as well as low Apgar scores on the 10-point rating scale of infants at delivery.

Genetic factors have been implicated in the diagnosis of ADHD for many years, and they appear to be a significant variable. Identical twins will share the ADHD trait, and a child who has ADHD usually has a close relative with this disorder. At least one-third of all men who had ADHD in their youth will father a child with ADHD. ADHD is more common among first-born males than later-born male or female siblings. Often the father has a positive history of ADHD, although at least one study has reported more first-degree relatives with ADHD among girls with ADHD than among boys with ADHD. It is clear that ADHD has a genetic component, and it is not gender linked. National studies of intergenerational ADHD are presently under way. Researchers at the National Institutes of Health are also tracking a gene that may be involved in transmitting ADHD in a small number of families with a genetic thyroid disorder (NIMH, 1999).

Suggestions that ADHD is caused by poor parenting are unfounded. However, ADHD can be aggravated by poor parenting and, like any other disorder, significant stress may increase the expression of what is already present—be it anxiety, depression, or hyperactivity. Family dynamics and the parental handling of ADHD-related behavior will influence family life as well as the behavior of the individual with ADHD. The parents will, understandably, have reactions to and make efforts to change or control ADHD-related behaviors and, in turn, the individual with ADHD will have reactions to and interpretations of the parental behavior (and form various ideas about himself or herself).

No clear evidence exists that food additives or diets high in sugar are etiologically related to ADHD. The Fiengold Diet and other natural-food diets have little or no impact on ADHD symptoms (for further discussion, see Wolraich et al., 1996). However, some individuals with a sensitivity to certain food substances may experience restlessness as a result of eating these foods.

Diversity Issues

Although biology is primarily responsible for the core behavioral symptoms of ADHD, the environment plays a significant role in providing the structure and feedback within which the individual behaves. Ethnic, gender, and socioeconomic group differences greatly influence the ADHD behavior exhibited by the individual. Thus, understanding the interaction between ADHD and the environmental situation and how this interaction affects therapeutic work are important elements in the treatment process (Gingerich et al., 1998).

INTERNATIONAL DIFFERENCES

International prevalence statistics for ADHD are difficult to compare because of changing syndrome criteria and variations in diagnostic methodology. Different cultures use different symptom terminology, diagnostic criteria, and treatment modalities. Some years back, the former Soviet Union classified children exhibiting these symptoms under the category "pathological development of childhood" (Barkley, 1998). In Germany, the terms were "psycho-organic syndrome" or "weakness of the brain functioning," and in France, the term was "cognitive disharmony" (Barkley, 1998).

Although ADHD is a relatively frequent diagnosis among school-age children in the United States, clinical perceptions of ADHD may be different in other countries even if uniform rating criteria are applied. For example, research has shown that clinicians from China and Indonesia tend to give higher ratings of hyperactivity than clinicians from Japan and the United States (Mann et al., 1992). Clinicians from various cultures may also significantly differ in reported use of assessment to diagnose ADHD. For example, U.S. clinicians use more assessment procedures than do Italian clinicians and, in beliefs about etiology, Italian clinicians put more importance on the role of environmental influences in ADHD, whereas U.S. clinicians believe more in organic influences (O'Leary, Vivian, & Cornaldi, 1984). Another study (Pendergast et al., 1988) also showed that use of the American Psychiatric Association's *DSM-III* criteria for ADHD generated more diagnoses than the WHO's (1978) *ICD-9* criteria for "Hyperkinetic Syndrome" for both U.S. and British clinicians. The effect was larger for British clinicians than it was for U.S. clinicians. Various studies have shown that prevalence rates vary cross-culturally due to variations in assessment and differences in sampling methodology and sample characteristics.

As a result of these international variations, clinicians in different cultures may either underdiagnose or overdiagnose ADHD because of cultural insensitivity and diagnostic bias, may misinterpret prevalence data, and may misjudge appropriate treatment modalities (Gingerich et al., 1998). Some researchers have argued that because societal tolerance for different behaviors vary across cultures and because unconventional behavior is defined by culture-specific norms rather than by some global uniform criteria, syndromes such as ADHD should be understood within the context of specific cultural environments and expectations (Chandra, 1993; Ideus, 1994).

ETHNIC VARIATIONS IN THE UNITED STATES

ADHD varies among the various ethnic populations within the United States. However, not many prevalence statistics are available, and available data may differ due to variations in assessment instruments and diagnostic strategies and to true differences in the frequency of the disorder. Studies in the 1970s comparing the prevalence of ADHD between ethnic minority and White children showed that ADHD rates as determined by teacher ratings were not uniform among ethnic minority children: African American children were rated as hyperactive more often than were White and Mexican American children. However, behavioral characteristics between children labeled as hyperactive across ethnic groups are not always similar; the quality of the activity that reflects the disorder may vary according to ethnic status, social class background, and teacher and student expectations (Gingerich et al., 1998).

Stevens (1981) found that school psychologists, parents, and teachers gave differential ratings to school children from different ethnic and socioeconomic backgrounds. School psychologists rated "lower class" boys as more hyperactive, with African American and Mexican American boys more so than lower class White boys. Teachers' ratings were more stable than those of school psychologists, and teachers rated Mexican American boys as less hyperactive than White and African American boys. Parents were more influenced by ethnic characteristics than by SES; they rated African American boys as more hyperactive than both Mexican American and White boys. Other research has suggested that the high diagnoses of ADHD among African American boys may be due to the large number of ethnic minority individuals living in highly stressful environments (Barbarin & Soler, 1993).

Some anecdotal evidence exists that ADHD behaviors tend to be viewed with less concern and tolerated more in some minority populations. Minority individuals with ADHD are less likely to enter the health care delivery system based on a diagnosis of ADHD. Rather, they are likely in a practitioner's office with other kinds of "disruptive" behavioral concerns such as oppositional defiant disorder and conduct disorder that may ultimately lead to an appropriate diagnosis of ADHD. The relationship between ethnicity and ADHD is understudied, and minority ethnic populations are severely underserved. Likewise, the relationship between SES and ADHD is not well understood, other than the observation that ADHD may be higher in lower socioeconomic groups (Gingerich et al., 1998).

GENDER

As noted earlier, attention deficits are much more likely to be diagnosed in males. Gender ratios of males to females vary from 2:1 to 10:1 (Ross & Ross, 1982); most research points to an approximate average of 6:1 for clinic-referred samples of U.S. children (Barkley, 1998). Epidemiological studies, however, report about a 3:1 proportion in the general U.S. child population (Szatmari et al., 1989).

The discrepancy between the gender ratio found in clinical samples and that found in the general population may be due to referral bias. In general, boys more often demonstrate their hyperactivity with aggressive, conduct-related maladaptive behaviors, and they may also have academic problems in school. Because these behaviors are more disruptive to parents and teachers, boys are more likely to be referred for evaluation and treatment. For girls, more severe behaviors must occur before a referral is made. Consequently, girls are often older than boys at the time of referral, and girls tend to be severely underdiagnosed. Some research suggests that girls are more often diagnosed with the inattentive form of ADHD rather than the hyperactive–impulsive form; because these symptoms are less aggressive and disruptive, they are less likely to be diagnosed.

As a general rule, in virtually all school settings, it is the disruptive child who is much more likely to come to the attention of teachers and school officials than the day-dreaming and inattentive child who is not performing up to potential. School-age girls who are hyperactive tend to exhibit their hyperactivity in ways very different from their male counterparts. Hyperactive school-age girls are more likely to be described as "talkative" or "very social." In fact, I have often heard these children described as resembling "Chatty Cathy," a talking doll that was popular with children several decades ago.

In both childhood and adulthood, females with ADHD have higher rates of depression and anxiety than those without ADHD. Some researchers have hypothesized that females are socialized to internalize ADHD symptoms such as anxiety and low self-esteem, whereas males are socialized to externalize ADHD symptoms of aggression and hyperactivity (Brown, Madan-Swain, & Baldwin, 1991).

Girls, as a group, exhibit a base level of inattention and hyperactivity lower than boys on many parent and teacher rating scales. This has been of concern, and the suggestion has been made that additional or modified gender-based criteria be used. These criteria, unfortunately, are only in the formulation stages of development. On the positive side, one reason why the ratio of boys to girls diagnosed with ADHD has been dropping in recent years is that clinicians have become more sensitive to the inattentive form of attention deficits. Additionally, the difference in the male–female ratio has been narrowing as the diagnostic criteria, increased sensitivity to gender-specific needs, and the availability of newer diagnostic questionnaires have enabled computerized assessment with both age- and gender-based norms.

Gender differences may exist in the life course of ADHD. Some studies have suggested that prognosis is better for girls with ADHD because they exhibit less hyperactivity-induced conduct problems. Onset of the disorder is generally later for girls than for boys, although hyperactive and restlessness symptoms may begin earlier with girls because they mature earlier physiologically than do boys. Other symptoms of ADHD worsen at puberty in women because hormonal variations can be very destructive on the regulation of attention and on the interaction of attention with mood and emotion.

The numbers of adult women and men with ADHD are about equal. Two factors may explain this change in the gender ratio. First, women are more likely to seek treatment, whereas men may ignore their symptoms and subsequent treatment. Second, it may be that, as adults, more women than men actually have ADHD, but the true number of female ADHD cases is masked by the high incidence of female depression. Thus, women are more likely to be misdiagnosed and treated for depression rather than properly diagnosed and treated for adult ADHD. Further research is needed to clarify this second factor.

Compared to non-ADHD control study participants, girls with ADHD become sexually active earlier, and boys with ADHD become sexually active later (Conners, personal communication, 1994, as cited in Arnold, 1996; Solden, 1995). Many young women with ADHD report episodes of hypersexual activity as teenagers (this issue is addressed in chapter 5). Women with ADHD tend to have a higher rate of teenage pregnancy (Barkley, personal communication, 1994, as cited in Arnold, 1996; Biederman, personal communication, 1994, as cited in Arnold, 1996; Loney, personal communication, 1994, as cited in Arnold, 1996). This finding could help explain the high rate of ADHD among adoptees.

There are no gender differences in response to medication management, and there is little to suggest that psychosocial treatments work better with one gender than with the other. However, adolescent girls with ADHD report more self-esteem issues, more of a sense of being "different" from peers, and more conflict with their mothers. These differences suggest that female teenagers and adults with ADHD may need more aggressive psychological and social approaches to treatment. Unfortunately, most studies on treatment approaches have focussed only on White males. In addition, because a woman's hormone makeup, from her premenopausal through her postmenopausal years, may influence ADHD, the effects of the estrous cycle on ADHD symptoms and its treatment are highly relevant and productive areas of study (Nadeau, 1996).

SOCIOECONOMIC STATUS

Many studies have found a link between SES and ADHD. However, it is not SES alone that affects the rate of ADHD, but rather the interaction of SES with other factors: fathers with low work classifications, parental divorce, minority status, stress, and other factors that affect low-SES populations. As is generally known, lower SES is associated with ethnic minority status, lower level of utilization of mental health services, poorer treatment compliance, poor prenatal care, and high incidence of substance abuse—all of which create considerable stress for individuals and families. Stress, in turn, is a significant risk factor for mental and behavioral health problems including ADHD. One study (Brown, Borden, Wynne, & Spunt, 1987) found that children with ADD from low-SES groups were equally likely to complete a 3-month treatment protocol as compared with children with ADD from other SES groups, they were less compliant with treatment, and they were also somewhat less compliant with medication than with psychotherapy. Thus, it is important for practitioners to be aware that individuals with lower SES are more vulnerable to ADHD, to anticipate noncompliance behavior in the treatment of this patient group, and to address treatment proactively.

ADHD in Adulthood

ADHD is not just a childhood disorder. It was previously believed that children eventually outgrow ADHD, but recent studies suggest that an estimated 30% to 70% of these children continue to show significant symptoms of the disorder into adulthood (Barkley, 1998; Wender, 1995). There is no such thing as adult-onset ADHD.

Because adult ADHD is the continuation of childhood ADHD into adulthood, childhood and adult ADHD are similar in symptomatology.

However, research indicates that, over the course of development, some symptoms change both in quality and quantity (G. Weiss & Hechtman, 1993; M. Weiss et al., 1999). Other symptoms remain the same but are manifested differently, because the tasks of adulthood are different. Some childhood symptoms may disappear, whereas other symptoms may become more disabling.

Hyperactivity as a symptom improves as most children grow older. Impulsivity changes quality—it also may diminish with age, but because it is a stable personality trait like aggression, it changes little as the child grows up. Attention problems remain the same but become more disabling as demands on the adult increase. Children with ADHD can pay attention to activities that interest them but become inattentive to activities that bore them. When a person with ADHD grows up, he or she has more choices for the activities that he or she may wish to engage in (M. Weiss et al., 1999).

The demands of the environment on children are different from the demands on adults. Therefore, the presenting problems will differ. "It is exactly the difference between what is expected of children and what is expected of adults that makes it hard to diagnose adult ADHD using childhood criteria, although the *DSM-IV* has attempted to bridge the gap" (M. Weiss et al., 1999, p. 26). Children must cope with the environmental rules laid out for them; adults have more choices. But adults also have greater responsibilities that require them to be generally well organized: They have to work, raise families, manage financial obligations, file their taxes, drive safely, keep appointments, and fulfill the numerous societal requirements for daily living. Adults with ADHD have problems in taking on and meeting most of these responsibilities (M. Weiss et al., 1999).

Core Symptoms

ADHD is characterized by the basic symptom clusters of inattention and hyperactivity–impulsivity. However, I believe that it is helpful to conceptualize ADHD as consisting of four core symptoms: inattention, impulsivity, (with or without) hyperactivity, and distractibility. These are the behaviors most often observed by and presented to the clinician either directly or in a derivative form, such as procrastination, forgetfulness, and disorganization. Symptom presentation can change over time; for example, hyperactivity in adults may be described as an internal sense of restlessness. Poor attention to tasks may be represented by the inability to keep a job.

INATTENTION

Individuals who are inattentive have difficulty keeping their minds on any one thing and quickly get bored with a task after only a few minutes. They may give effortless, automatic attention to activities that they enjoy, but they often have difficulty focusing deliberate, conscious attention to organizing and completing a task or learning something new (NIMH, 1999). Such inattention may be reported as forgetfulness, poor organization, poor concentration, and poor time management. They may withdraw from or feel awkward in social situations; become easily depressed by stress or feelings of being overwhelmed; are often disorganized and unable to complete tasks, even those they enjoy or are in their best interest to complete; and experience their mind wandering. They tend to be "attentive" to internal events such as their own thoughts and fantasies, or they may daydream, having little or no idea of what goes on around them.

IMPULSIVITY

Individuals who are overly impulsive have difficulty curbing their immediate reactions or thinking before acting. Thus, they may blurt out inappropriate comments or make angry outbursts; engage in unnecessary high-risk activities; engage in illegal behavior such as breaking driving rules, gambling, and using drugs; and present hypersexuality problems. Impulsivity may also be manifested in such behavior as "binge buying"; overusing credit cards; or collecting large quantities of such things as baseball cards, comic books, dolls, and so forth. Impulsive adults may appear impatient, verbally abusive, and unable to read nonverbal cues and behaviors of others around them. As a consequence, they are seen as social outsiders and may well have serious deficits in social skills and dealing with people.

DISTRACTIBILITY

Individuals with ADHD become easily distracted by irrelevant sights and sounds. Every change in the environment—a movement or a sound—draws their attention. Thus, they are unable to work in distracting environments and cannot filter out background sights and sounds. They are constantly forgetting things, items, or appointments. They have compliance problems, may behave passive–aggressively, and rarely follow instructions carefully and completely. They also tend to be underachievers throughout most of their lives as measured against their given abilities, intelligence, and education. Given all of these behavioral deficits, it is not surprising that individuals with ADHD often experience problems at work; in their marital, sexual, and family relationships; and even with the law.

HYPERACTIVITY

Hyperactivity may or may not be present in the individual with ADHD. Hyperactivity in adults may not necessarily be overt motor movements, although some will show both leg and hand restlessness. More frequently it is experienced as a feeling of inner tension (not anxiety) when one is required by the task or the situation to remain seated or stay still for extended periods of time. As one adult with ADHD said to me, the feeling is like holding your breath; you can only do it for so long and then you have to breathe. Many adults with a hyperactive component feel intensely restless and may be fidgety. They cannot work quietly at one task but may try to do several things at once, bouncing from one activity to the next to discharge energy and their feeling of inner tension.

Of course not everyone who exhibits these core behavior symptoms necessarily has ADHD. To some extent, all adults exhibit some or all of these behaviors at one point or another. To determine whether a person has ADHD, clinicians consider several criteria: Are these behaviors excessive, long-term, and pervasive? Do they tend to be continuous problems rather than temporary responses to a temporary situation? Do the behaviors occur in several settings or only in one specific place? Thus, the individual's pattern of behavior must be compared against a set of criteria and characteristics of the disorder as determined by the *DSM-IV*, diagnostic screening questionnaires, and computer-based tests.

THREE ASPECTS OF ATTENTION

It may be helpful to conceptualize attention into three aspects: sustained, divided, and alternating. The first step in "paying attention" is selecting the right stimulus in the environment that one wants to attend to. Staying with that stimulus over time is the sustaining component or focus. In the case of the individual with ADHD, the problem is not just paying attention, but paying attention over time or maintaining sustained attention over time. Imagine the consequences if an air traffic controller at Chicago's O'Hare Airport was experiencing this inattention problem.

In addition to sustaining attention, people unaffected by ADHD must be able to divide attention between competing but relevant stimuli, for example, simultaneously driving and listening to the radio. But notice what happens when the driver sees an accident or hears a siren on the road. Attention is quickly diverted to the urgent stimuli, and sometimes the driver may not recall what was on the radio. This is the third aspect of attention—shifting. That is, when the siren is heard, rather than dividing attention between the highway and radio, the attention has fully shifted to the road. Thus, each attention task the driver engages in is a factor of attention, and problems can occur in any or all of these factors, ultimately affecting the global concept of attention. This explains why individuals with ADHD appear slow, disinterested, and easily bored; their attention keeps shifting or alternating, with the behavior producing no useful end results.

Conclusion

ADHD is not a disorder confined to children; there are millions of adults, likely equally divided between men and women, who have attention deficits. Many have struggled with this problem for years with varying degrees of success, some with a variety of compensatory strategies. Childhood ADHD symptoms tend to change over time, and the criteria needed to make a diagnosis may need to be altered as the individual grows to adulthood. I strongly believe that as clinicians, we should not be constrained by the rigid application of *DSM-IV* criteria. There are specific and general diagnostic screening questionnaires and computer-based tests that can be utilized with adults (they will be discussed in later chapters). The impact of ADHD in adulthood is profound, as it can produce almost unrelenting problems in their personal, social, familial, and occupational lives. It is also important to recognize that, like children with ADHD, adults with ADHD do not experience symptoms all of the time. It depends on the adult, the situation, the time, and the context.

References and Resources

American Psychiatric Association. (1994). *Diagnostic and statistical manual of mental disorders* (4th ed.). Washington, DC: Author.

Arnold, L. E. (1996). Sex differences in ADHD: Conference summary. *Journal of Abnormal Psychology, 24*(5), 555–569.

Barbarin, O. A., & Soler, R. E. (1993). Behavioral, emotional, and academic adjustment in a national probability sample of African American children: Effects of age, gender, and family structure. *Journal of Black Psychology, 19*, 423–446.

Barkley, R. A. (1997). Behavioral inhibition, sustained attention, and executive functions: Constructing a unifying theory of ADHD. *Psychological Bulletin, 121,* 65–86.

Barkley, R. A. (1998). *Attention-deficit-hyperactivity disorder: A handbook for diagnosis and treatment* (2nd ed.). New York: Guilford Press.

Baumgaertel, A., Wolraich, M. L., & Dietrich, M. (1995). Comparison of diagnostic criteria for attention deficit disorders in a German elementary school sample. *Journal of the American Academy of Child and Adolescent Psychiatry, 34,* 629–638.

Brown, R. T., Borden, K. A., Wynne, M. E., & Spunt, A. L. (1987). Compliance with pharmacological and cognitive treatments for attention deficit disorder. *Journal of the American Academy of Child and Adolescent Psychiatry, 26,* 521–526.

Brown, R. T., Madan-Swain, A., & Baldwin, K. (1991). Gender differences in a clinic-referred sample of attention-deficit-disordered children. *Child Psychiatry and Human Development, 22,* 111–129.

Cantwell, D. P. (1996). Attention deficit disorder: A review of the past 10 years. *Journal of the American Academy of Child and Adolescent Psychiatry, 35,* 978–987.

Chandra, P. S. (1993). Cross-cultural psychiatry and children with deviant behaviors. *American Journal of Psychiatry, 150,* 1279–1280.

Cook, J. (1997). *The book of positive quotations.* Minneapolis, MN: Fairview Press.

Gingerich, K. J., Turnock, P., Litfin, J. K., & Rosen, L. A. (1998). Diversity and attention deficit hyperactivity disorder. *Journal of Clinical Psychology, 54,* 415–428.

Hallowell, E. M., & Ratey, J. J. (1994). *Driven to distraction.* New York: Simon & Schuster.

Hunt, R. D. (1997). Nosology, neurobiology, and clinical patterns of ADHD in adults. *Psychiatric Annals, 27,* 572–580.

Ideus, K. (1994). Cultural foundations of ADHD: A sociological analysis. *Therapeutic Care and Education, 3,* 173–192.

Mann, E. M., Ikeda, Y., Mueller, C. W., Takahashi, A., Tao, K. T., Humris, E., Li, B. L., & Chin, D. (1992). Cross-cultural differences in rating hyperactive-disruptive behaviors in children. *American Journal of Psychiatry, 149,* 1539–1542.

Nadeau, K. G. (1996). *Adventures in fast forward: Life, love, and work for the ADD adult.* New York: Brunner-Mazel.

National Institute of Mental Health. (1999). *Attention deficit hyperactivity disorder.* Available online at www.nimh.nih.gov/publicat/adhd.htm

O'Leary, K. D., Vivian, D., & Cornaldi, C. (1984). Assessment and treatment of "hyperactivity" in Italy and the United States. *Journal of Clinical Child Psychology, 13,* 56–60.

Pendergast, M., Taylor, E., Rappoport, L., Bartko, J., Donnelly, M., Zametkin, A., Ahearn, M. B., Dunn, G., & Wieselberg, H. M. (1988). The diagnosis of childhood hyperactivity: A U.S.-U.K. cross-national study of DSM-III and ICD-9. *Journal of Child Psychiatry and Psychology and Allied Disciplines, 29,* 289–300.

Ross, D. M., & Ross, S. A. (1982). *Hyperactivity: Research, theory, and action.* New York: Wiley.

Solden, S. (1995). *Women with attention deficit disorder.* Grass Valley, CA: Underwood Books.

Stevens, G. (1981). Bias in the attribution of hyperkinetic behavior as a function of ethnic identification and socioeconomic status. *Psychology in the Schools, 18,* 99–106.

Szatmari, P., Offord, D. R., & Boyle, M. H. (1989). Ontario child health study: Prevalence of attention deficit disorder with hyperactivity. *Journal of Child Psychology and Psychiatry, 30,* 219–230.

Weiss, G., & Hechtman, L. (1993). *Hyperactive children grown up: ADHD in children, adolescents and adulthood* (2nd ed.). New York: Guilford Press.

Weiss, M., Hechtman, L. T., & Weiss, G. (1999). *ADHD in adulthood: A guide to current theory, diagnosis, and treatment.* Baltimore: Johns Hopkins University Press.

Wender, P. H. (1995). *Attention-deficit-hyperactivity disorders in adulthood.* New York: Oxford University Press.

Wolraich, M. L., Hannah, J. N., Pinnock, T. Y., Baumgaertel, A., & Brown, J. (1996). The effect of sugar on behavior or cognition in children: A meta-analysis. *Journal of the American Medical Association, 274,* 1617–1621.

World Health Organization. (1978). *International classification of diseases* (9th ed.). Geneva, Switzerland: Author.

Patient Presentation | 3

The work will teach you how to do it.
—Estonian proverb

Adults with ADHD usually come to the clinician's office with symptoms and problems that masquerade as other diagnoses. These other symptoms generally become the focus of treatment, and the ADHD is missed. These adults are seeking professional help about a variety of personal problems—their marriages or significant relationships, parenting skills, relationships with peers, academic or work performance, and even their use of leisure time.

Being unaware of their ADHD, many adults seek help for feeling anxious or depressed, feeling overwhelmed by life's demands, being unable to handle stress appropriately, or feeling that "things aren't right." In questioning during the initial interview, the clinician is often able to discern a lack of focus, disorganization, and constant turmoil in the patient's day-to-day life.

The behavioral symptoms of adult ADHD revolve around the four core symptoms of inattention, impulsivity, (with or without) hyperactivity, and distractibility (discussed in chapter 2). The individual with ADHD may present these behaviors directly or in a derivative form. This chapter discusses the various behaviors and symptoms that an undiagnosed adult with ADHD may present to a clinician when seeking professional help and the settings in which these behaviors can be problems.

ADHD Behaviors and Symptoms

DISTRACTIBILITY

In adulthood, attention difficulties are not as evident as they are in childhood, and the adult patient is not likely to spontaneously mention to a clinician that he or she has attention problems. This is because most adults with ADHD are no longer in school and rarely find themselves in situations requiring their sustained attention over extended periods of time. Adults generally have more of a choice about whether to engage in attention-demanding activities that increase their stress levels; adults with ADHD will usually choose to avoid such activities whenever possible. Nonetheless, adults with ADHD do experience attention difficulties to a far greater extent than adults without ADHD, and these difficulties interfere with the patient's daily performance.

The symptoms that characterize an adult's attention problems may be any of the following: distractibility, inattention to details, inability to complete tasks, poor planning ability, disorganization, resistance to tasks requiring concentration, forgetfulness, and the tendency to lose or misplace personal items (Nadeau, 1996). ADHD is also associated with short-term memory problems such as easily forgetting a supervisor's verbal instructions; having difficulty recalling what was just read; forgetting or being late for appointments and meetings; forgetting plans; and losing or misplacing one's wallet, keys, and other personal items (Wender, 1995).

The young college adult most likely will have persistent attention problems that will affect his or her school performance and thus will remain the "underachiever" that he or she may have been in grade school (Wender, 1995). He or she may report being unable to focus on

FRANK AND ERNEST reprinted by permission of Newspaper Enterprise Association, Inc.

reading and school work, having a very limited attention span in the classroom, and finding routine school work boring.

The husband with ADHD may find it hard to keep his mind on his wife's conversation just as he had problems listening to his teachers' lectures. Not only is the adult with ADHD inattentive, but she or he is often interpersonally impulsive, interrupting speakers and thus annoying them.

Individuals who present initially as possibly having a passive–aggressive personality (or the occasional oppositional defiant personality) should also be screened for ADHD. More detailed interviewing is needed. Such individuals are often described by others as deliberately sabotaging or out to do mischief. They themselves may describe their behavior in ways that appear passive–aggressive or oppositionally defiant. Complaints like "My husband asked me to pick up his dry cleaning, and I didn't"; "I can't ask my husband to do two things at once, or one or both won't get done"; "I have to talk to her like she is 4 years old"; and "Why can't he do just one thing I ask him to the first time I ask him?" are a few examples. These individuals may also exhibit self-defeating behaviors. As one of my patients described it, he could not "win for losing." Despite his best efforts he could not "get ahead of the game." Such individuals also may reveal a history of interpersonal insensitivity, difficulty with interpreting the subtle nuances of other people's behavior, and an inability to recognize nonverbal cues.

A common denominator among these personality styles is a problem with memory. Many individuals with ADHD have significant difficulty accessing working memory so, although events have transpired, they do not have consistent capacity to access those memories and use them for future reference. If the memory trace is not accessed, then the commitment or promised event cannot occur. Once lost in memory the proposed action does not exist in their subjective perception of reality. The result is more than "forgetting," because, for those with ADHD, the event or action does not exist in their memory and therefore cannot happen. Indeed, the failure to honor commitments causes trouble for adults with ADHD. Not surprisingly, some become suspicious, as they are "positive" that they did not say or promise what others say that they did. To make matters worse, those around adults with ADHD may view them with disdain because of these undependable and untrustworthy behaviors.

Case Vignette: Marie

Marie, age 44 and a real estate agent, presented with problems of insomnia and general anxiety. She is married to an engineer and has two teenage children. Although the marriage has been reasonably successful and the children are doing well in school, Marie's husband constantly complains about how disorganized she is and about their disorganized household. Being an engineer, he believes that his wife should just "do it and be organized about doing it."

She worries through the early hours of the morning about her chores for the next day: who has to be taken where, what real estate appointments need to be made, and so forth. Sometimes she makes lists when she cannot sleep. She wakes in the morning fatigued and dreading the day ahead. Marie would make more lists during the day, but the activities listed were hardly ever completed. The last few months before the consultation, she stopped making lists because "the list only provided me with additional grief because it was a list of what I didn't get done." (As an aside, lists are often very helpful in organizing adults with ADHD, but this is a good illustration of when that intervention strategy is poorly implemented and becomes counterproductive.)

Marie would sometimes forget to pick up clients to look at properties. On one occasion she neglected to present a contract to the sellers, so the house was sold to another family instead of to her buyers. Sometimes Marie felt so overwhelmed that she would simply sit in the bedroom and cry.

Her disorganization contributed to her stress level, which affected her already impaired coping skills. The disorganization caused the insomnia, dysphoria, and anxiety. Her husband's advice, offered from an engineer's highly organized way of thinking, further aggravated Marie's anxiety.

Marie's history is consistent with ADHD. She was an honor student in elementary school, but her grades slipped a little in middle school, and by high school she was barely a C student. She did fine in her elementary and middle grades because the tasks were simpler and more defined and the classes were not large. However, her high school was too big and too busy for her. School work increased demands on her already overstressed attention capacity, which precipitated her declining grades. She began experimenting with drugs as a way of handling the stress. When the school suggested an evaluation to determine why this capable student was having so many problems, her parents objected, saying that Marie "just had to apply herself more." Following her parents' advice only contributed to increasing her stress level, as the extra effort produced no improvement. She graduated from high school feeling demoralized and like a failure and with poor self-esteem.

Treatment consisted of a collaborative arrangement between her therapist and the primary care physician, who provided the stimulant medication. Bibliotherapy and psychotherapy were provided by the therapist. The therapist saw Marie and her husband together for extensive discussion about the nature and course of ADHD. Marie then came for individual therapy to work on self-esteem issues, followed by several joint sessions again with her husband to finalize suggested interventions to be made in the home. Her husband took over more of the child-rearing responsibilities and car-pooling tasks. Treatment was discontinued.

Three years later when her oldest daughter was to be married, Marie came back to treatment briefly seeking help on how to manage the planning of the wedding. Once again, the impending event was placing more demands on her attention than she could handle. But this time, Marie decided to take charge of the situation and went to her therapist to learn new coping strategies for dealing with the new stressor.

Marie is an example of what is typical in the lifetime treatment of adult ADHD. In the life course of the person with ADHD new situations arise (career, marriage and divorce, children, relocation) that require therapeutic intervention. The patient will be seen for a number of sessions intermittently as the need arises over his or her life span.

Case Vignette: Carl

Carl, age 42, was referred by his primary care physician to confirm the physician's diagnosis of manic depression before starting him on medication. Carl presented as a fast-talking, cheerful, married man with one child who is attending college. He is a fairly successful insurance agent running his own agency; his wife is the office manager. He comes across in the clinical interview as a gregarious and charming man who sees nothing problematic with his behavior, but he came for consultation at the insistence of his wife and his primary care physician. She does his scheduling and reminds him of his appointments; she would call him up to 15 times a day on his cellular phone to remind him of where he needed to be next. Carl never objected to these calls and found them "helpful."

It was difficult to pick up anything of significance from his childhood and teenage years or even from his academic history, as he would brush it aside and say that it was all a big blur. At the end of the first interview it was almost impossible to determine with confidence whether Carl had bipolar disorder, hypomania, or ADHD.

On the second interview his wife was present, and she gave a clearer picture of the extent of his behavior. He had problems focusing even on simple tasks like reading a newspaper or watching a 30-minute television show. With further probing, Carl admitted that he forgot to do things despite reminders, was always behind with paperwork, and missed deadlines. He had occasional problems with details on the underwriting of some of the insurance policies. His wife further reported that their son went to a liberal arts college with a student population of about 1,000 because he always did better in smaller, well-structured classes.

With this information, it soon became evident that Carl did not have bipolar disorder or hypomania but had significant attention deficits, which were subsequently confirmed by questionnaires and computerized assessment. A primary care physician initially prescribed a stimulant for Carl. He experienced significant side effects with the first stimulant, so the physician referred him to a psychiatrist for medication management.

To manage his ADHD-related behavior, Carl bought a portable computerized time management program for scheduling his appointments. In his office, he had 90 minutes of "protected time" each day to catch up on paperwork. During this time, he would take no calls or have any interruptions. At home, his wife blocked off some time for discussion of important family matters using the "I talk, you listen; then you talk, I listen" approach. In this approach the person listening cannot speak or rebut until the person talking is finished, then the process is reversed. Personalities are kept out of the discussion, and the speakers stay focused on issues. Only "I messages," are permissible, as in "I get upset when I eat dinner alone" as opposed to "Why can't you be home on time for dinner?"

IMPULSIVITY

As with children, adults with ADHD cannot delay gratification and also have a low level of tolerance. They are impatient. They act impulsively —at the spur of the moment and without thinking. They even make important decisions without sufficient information or reflection on the consequences of their actions. Such behavior manifests itself at work, at home, in interpersonal relationships, and in problem solving. Adults with ADHD, in comparison with clinical or control groups, often self-report symptoms of poor impulse control, such as difficulty awaiting turns; poor inhibition in their emotional reactions to others, such as blurting out answers and interrupting others; difficulty exercising impulse control while driving, such as speeding; and difficulty with finances, such as impulsively spending money (Barkley, 1998).

Case Vignette: Roddy

Roddy, age 23, was referred by the court and his attorney for evaluation. Roddy had a history of reckless driving and speeding. He had gone to driving school twice. He lost his license for a period of time and was allowed to drive only to and from work. Shortly after his license was reinstated, he got another speeding ticket. At each court appearance, he was distressed and could not offer the court any explanation for his ongoing difficulties. His last court appearance was for "drag racing" in the early morning on an interstate highway at speeds in excess of 100 miles per hour.

History revealed that Roddy had been an underachieving student; the school regularly informed his parents that he could do better. Throughout his education, Roddy was frequently in the principal's office for inappropriate behaviors such as setting off firecrackers in the boys' restroom; taking his penis out of his trousers during class; and riding his bike in the school, including riding it down the stairs. He was also a risk taker who sought novel stimulation. As a teenager he enjoyed rock climbing and would climb where others feared to go. He tried hang gliding, parasailing, and bungee jumping.

Roddy was not diagnosed with ADHD until he was referred. All of the data supported the diagnosis: history, school records, personal rating scales and testing, and parents' rating scales. He refused all treatment other than medication, saying that there was nothing wrong with him that the medicine could not fix. Unfortunately, such was not the case. He discontinued his medication, as he did not keep his follow-up appointment with the prescribing physician, and he was later incarcerated for violating his driving probation.

AFFECTIVE LABILITY

Affective lability, being dysphoric at one time and overexcited the next, is a significant symptom of childhood ADHD that carries through into adulthood. Adults with ADHD often experience mood shifts, "ups and downs" that occur both autonomously and in reaction to daily experiences. The ups are usually like the excitement of the overstimulated child rather than the elation associated with euphoria or hypomania. The downs are often described by patients as discontent or boredom rather than as mood alterations related to depression such as anhedonia (Wender, 1995).

Individuals with ADHD may complain of sleep and appetite problems and of being tired and listless. They may express feelings of many personal failures; they carry a history of bad experiences like a heavy burden. When mood lability is present, it is not of the same severity seen in major depression or bipolar disorder, nor does it last as long. This lability may last for a few hours or a day, and it is not sustained, with mood level returning to a personal baseline and then shifting again. This type of depression, often seen in undiagnosed ADHD cases, is generally the consequence of years of unfulfilled promise and potential. Because depression tends to run in families in which ADHD is present, the ADHD can be overlooked. In addition, an individual may be treated for depression for months before the ADHD symptomatology that drives the depression becomes evident. Careful probing of those behaviors that are the consequences of inattention, distractibility, and impulsivity with or without hyperactivity is needed to cue the clinical interview or intervention toward attention deficits.

Individuals with ADHD may engage in high-risk behaviors as an antidote for boredom. Although not quite living on the edge, they do enjoy a "fast" lifestyle, which can get them into significant difficulty with family and friends, legal authorities, and personal finances. Courts and lawyers often refer high-energy individuals who have had ongoing brushes with the law for consultation and treatment. These individuals may appear to be hypomanic, showing rapid speech and some flightiness in their thinking along with restlessness and irritability. The same presentation may be seen in adults with ADHD. However, people with hypomania will have more ongoing and enduring inappropriate cheerfulness and euphoria, whereas adults with ADHD will tend to exhibit frequent mood changes from euphoria to boredom to dysphoria. People with hypomania generally do not complain or seem concerned about their symptoms and problems, whereas adults with ADHD more often are perplexed and even confused by their behavior and symptoms. People with ADHD also have an increased need for stimulation, which makes them prone to risk-taking behavior.

Affective lability also produces excessive anger and an explosive temper. Individuals with ADHD often calm down quickly between outbursts, but some are chronically irritable, frightened when they lose control, and are unable to appreciate the negative consequences of their outbursts (e.g., the destruction of personal property, financial ruin and, most important, damage to significant social relationships; Wender, 1995).

Anyone who presents with a history of alcohol or drug abuse also could have ADHD. Substance abuse is a common outcome among impulsive and overactive teenagers as well as among adults who were never treated for their ADHD in their childhood. The potential for addiction is high among individuals with a history of high risk taking, impulsivity, and elevated activity level.

Case Vignette: Clarissa

Clarissa, age 48, presented with depressed mood and constricted affect. She had a sad look on her face and sighed audibly throughout the initial interview. Her chief complaint was that "nothing has ever gone right." She stated, with grave concern and some pain, "I know where I want to go; I just can't seem to get there."

She described a history of sadness and depression beginning in late childhood and continuing to the present. With much difficulty she was able to complete high school and then junior college and ultimately completed her education at a small liberal arts college. She dropped out of junior college twice and out of the liberal arts college three times prior to being awarded her degree in English. Over the years she has had several serious relationships with men, none of which lasted because, as Clarissa believes, she could not make a commitment.

She recalled that in college she found herself doing better when she sat in the front row directly before the instructor rather than in the back, where she would daydream and worry about other things. She thought that her concentration improved in the front row because the teacher would be looking at her. Problems in concentration varied from day to day and week to week but with no discernible pattern.

Her grandmother, by her mother's report and as Clarissa remembered, was "a little off" and seemed to be depressed, although no formal diagnosis was made or treatment instituted.

Clarissa showed no evidence of elevated activity; indeed, she could be better described as hypoactive in her lethargy and sad appearance. Suicidal ideation was absent, as were appetite and sleeping problems. No other significant findings were evident on mental status. Screening questionnaires and computerized assessment indicated a nonhyperactive, primarily inattentive individual whose response to chronic underachievement and lack of success were the breeding ground for her depression.

Because of her low energy and anhedonia, the drug selected by the prescribing physician was an antidepressant. Individual psychotherapy focused on self-esteem and allowing expression of anger and anguish over not being diagnosed earlier. She finally expressed a sense of relief over being able to account for her lifelong interpersonal and academic problems. Books and articles about ADHD were recommended, and she read them. She also became active in the local support group for ADHD adults. As she said many times, "It's just nice to know I am not the only one out there like me!"

Case Vignette: Harry

Harry, age 38, a high school graduate, is the father of two daughters by different wives but divorced from both. He lives alone, although he has an on-again–off-again relationship with a divorced woman with no children. He presented with "nothing makes me happy."

In the clinical interview, Harry described a lifetime of "just getting by." He struggled his way through school but was never a behavior problem. He had a few friends and dated occasionally. His employment history was fairly consistent. He had been in the same job as an electrician for 8 years. Harry reported, in passing, that over the years his coworkers tended to avoid teaming up with him, and he found himself, more often than not, working alone on the job. Harry was not sure why that was, although he admitted that at times he got "grouchy."

When asked if there was anything he enjoyed, he said "not really." He added, "not even my birthdays when I was a kid." Harry was showing anhedonic qualities seen among many children and adults with attention deficits. Life did not give him much pleasure, not even events that others celebrate and consider joyful.

A fruitful line of questioning is how such people were treated and disciplined as children; they were often unresponsive to the usual parental rewards and punishments. This was true for Harry. He admitted that it did not matter to him to be spanked or grounded. In fact, he recalled musing about what would happen if he were "grounded for life."

Harry had ADHD with anhedonia. A multifaceted treatment plan was put in place. Stimulant medication was tried first and succeeded not only in increasing his attention, but also in taking the edge off his irritability. Then an attempt was made to educate Harry about the nature and course of his ADHD. At his request, the woman he was dating accompanied him to a session. She was understanding and supportive and wanted to know how she could help. This appeared to lift from Harry the burden of having ADHD and suffering alone, and their relationship became closer. Harry was not a reader and did not want to join a support group. Harry's girlfriend read the educational material and then discussed it with him. This seemed to work. Gradually, Harry made friends at work, mostly among new employees who did not know his history.

HYPERACTIVITY

Symptoms of hyperactive or restless behavior are often present in adults with ADHD, such as difficulties with fidgeting, excessive speech, and a subjective sense of restlessness (Barkley, 1998). In contrast to adult study participants without ADHD, participants with ADHD were more likely to fidget with their hands or feet, had difficulty remaining seated, and verbalized more than others (Murphy & Barkley, 1996). Adults with ADHD may self-describe as always needing to be on the go and feeling more comfortable with stimulating activities rather than with sedentary ones. In addition, their excessive talking, clowning, repartee, or other ways of dominating conversation may mask a basic inability to engage in give-and-take conversation, causes inappropriate social behavior at parties, and even interferes with developing intimacy (Weiss, Hechtman, & Weiss, 1999).

LEARNING DISABILITY

One additional parameter needs to be considered in evaluating an adult for ADHD: learning disability (LD). Many adults will enter a clinician's office defining themselves as having an LD. That self-pronouncement, even with an earlier evaluation, should be carefully reviewed by clinicians, keeping in mind the possibility of undiagnosed ADHD.

There are three possible outcomes with respect to ADHD and LD as children grow into adulthood. First, some children grow up with no LD problems. Second, some children will have clear cases of LD that run parallel to ADHD; to the extent that the ADHD symptoms are addressed so, too, will there be some improvement in their LD problems. Finally, some children grow up believing they have an LD when actually their LD is the sequelae of an undiagnosed ADHD. This last group of adults, as children, may have been told they had an LD when, in fact, ADHD symptoms may be the cause of their learning problems. As the ADHD is controlled and addressed, LD will take on a new meaning.

In many instances, the LD may stem from educational gaps in their acquired knowledge, and specific tutoring or other academic interventions can ameliorate these problems. A case example is the adult who knew algebra but could not do fractions. In the course of her ADHD treatment, focused relearning of the rules of fractions ended her mathematics LD.

The impact that a correct diagnosis can make on a patient's career choice, advancement, and self-esteem is most profound. Those who work regularly with attention deficits may soon gain a reputation of being able to "cure" LD, because helping the patient control inattention, hyperactivity, and distractibility implies controlling the very symptoms that may be the basis of one's learning problems. Thus, practitioners should be sensitive in evaluating adults with an LD diagnosis who have never been evaluated for ADHD.

ADHD in Specific Relationships and Settings

MARITAL AND OTHER RELATIONSHIPS

In marriages or other significant relationships, ADHD, whether diagnosed in one or both partners, can create a chaotic and potentially hostile environment. Either one of a couple in a relationship may have an explosive temper or dramatic mood swing as a result of misinterpreting or misunderstanding the other's nonverbal cues. Such emotional outbursts place significant stress on the viability and durability of the relationship and can even lead to domestic violence.

ADHD behavior may also affect sexual relationships. For women, there may be episodes of hypersexuality (and to a lesser degree, hyposexuality), with this most typically occurring in their teenage or early adult years. As adults, women with attention deficits experience problems of focus during lovemaking. Some are distracted by anticipated events of the next day, the telephone ringing, or other intrusions.

Men with ADHD also can experience problems in lovemaking and intimacy. They can become easily bored or distracted during lovemaking, and they can be totally insensitive to their partner's physical and emotional needs. Some men cannot appreciate foreplay and postintercourse intimacy and bonding. As one patient in my practice complained of her husband with ADHD, "It's one, two, three. Kiss me, feel me, mount me." Because men with ADHD often experience boredom and high stimulation, they may be prone to engaging in risky sexual behavior that include sexual diversions and multiple partners.

One of the most common complaints about a partner who has ADHD is disorganization. Disorganized behavior leads to problems in completing tasks at home and on the job, and it ultimately affects marital and family relationships. It also leads to problems in parenting. Adults with poor follow-through have difficulty trying to remain reasonably consistent with their children. Adults bring to parenting their experiences as a child, and a parent who carries his or her childhood ADHD symptoms to adulthood without benefit of treatment is not likely to have positive childhood experiences to guide him or her in child-rearing endeavors. This carryover behavior may express itself as being overdemanding on one occasion and overlenient the next. Such behavior often leads to arguments between the parents on how their children should be raised.

Case Vignette: Lois and Ronnie

Lois and Ronnie are in their early 30s and have been married 6 years. They have one child, Annie, age 2. Both are college educated and have successful careers as mid-level managers in separate large manufacturing firms. They were seeing a psychologist together to work on their "communication problems."

After several sessions, the discussion turned to Lois's problems with details. Ronnie often talked to Lois about getting things done but was not overly upset when, at the last moment, he would have to step in to handle important matters affecting the household or their daughter's day care. Lois revealed that she had had ADHD as a child but had "outgrown it" and stopped treatment when she was 14.

The discussion turned to the sexual side of their marriage. Lois complained that their sex life was boring. Ronnie replied that it was not very good for him either. There followed many complaints and countercomplaints, with both becoming defensive. However, the psychologist could not elicit any history of specific sexual problems, and both admitted that there were times when their lovemaking was very good. Ultimately, Ronnie's complaint was that on some occasions he felt like he was making love to a mannequin. Lois's response was that she was often not in the mood. The therapist asked them to report the next time this happened and suggested that Ronnie ask Lois what was on her mind.

In a later session, Lois admitted that her mind would drift to things she had to take care of the next day. She had not realized this. She could identify ADHD behaviors in herself as an adult but believed that she had actually outgrown the disorder. She thought she was just not a detail person. Besides, Ronnie was "always there to save the day."

Lois agreed to again take stimulant medication; she preferred something that could be taken once or at most twice a day, because her life was too busy to continually remember her medication. She took the medication on weekdays only, feeling no need for it on weekends, when she was free from the stress of her job and the day care center. Communication between Lois and Ronnie seemed to improve significantly. Furthermore, both were happy to report that their lovemaking had improved.

Case Vignette: Charles and Lydia

Charles and Lydia are in their late 20s and have been married for 3 years. They were referred through an employee assistant program (EAP) to a social worker with extensive experience in couples therapy. After several sessions, the social worker referred Charles to a psychologist for potential ADHD.

The social worker explained to the clinician that Lydia reported sometimes feeling, when talking to Charles, like she was talking to a wall, and on many occasions Charles really had no idea what she was saying. His responses were often unrelated to the topic. When this was pointed out to him, he often became angry. Sometimes he would storm out of the house. On one occasion, he threw a glass of soda against the wall. He soon was apologetic and repentant, but the behaviors would reappear during the next altercation.

Lydia complained that she was often "acting like his mother." Things did not get done around their newly acquired home unless, as Charles put it, Lydia "nagged me to death." Charles would forget to stop at the store to pick up groceries, forget to do the lawn work, and fail to pay bills on time and thus accrued expensive late charges on credit cards. Lydia's suggestion that she take over the bill paying was met with an angry outburst from Charles. Arguments would often end in a love-making session, but the lovemaking was unsatisfactory to both of them. Lydia stated that there was no passion; Charles, although sexually satisfied, recognized that something was missing, especially when he looked at Lydia after intercourse.

Charles was evaluated for ADHD, which was confirmed. His behavior is an excellent example of disorganization based on poor memory storage and retrieval. Lydia could not win; if she "nagged" he got angry; if she did not remind him, things did not get done. Charles just did not get around to doing the things that he wanted to do and knew that he should do. This extended to things he enjoyed; for example, he sometimes forgot to meet friends to go fishing. His genuine perplexity over his recalcitrant behavior was most significant; this discriminates it from avoidance or passive–aggressiveness.

Case Vignette: Roy and Carol

Roy and Carol are in their late 30s. They have two children, Roy III, age 8, whose nickname is Trip, and John, age 6. Carol and Roy came in for consultation because, as Carol stated, "I can write the book on chaos theory." Roy, on the other hand, smiled and gave the interviewer a bewildered look. Carol described a large number of complaints.

By all accounts, Roy is a good carpenter. When John was born he decided to add a bedroom to the house. That project was interrupted when Roy got a promotion. Since they could then afford a second car, Roy decided that he would add a two-car garage. About a year and a half after that project was started, Roy decided that it was time to enlarge the family room, as both boys needed a larger play area. About another year later, with the family room still not finished, Roy decided that they needed an additional bathroom and proceeded to knock out part of the kitchen wall to access the plumbing. After 6 years none of the projects had been completed.

As Carol delineated all of this, Roy rarely commented. At the end he said, "I'm working on it." Carol was clearly frustrated by Roy's behavior, but Roy continued to be oblivious to the consequences of his inability to complete one job before starting another.

Roy's mother stated that Trip is the spitting image of his father. Trip, by observation, has ADHD, which in all of this chaos has probably gone unnoticed. In dealing with Trip, as well as John, Roy vacillates from being very harsh and demanding immediate obedience to dismissing their behavior by saying that "boys will be boys."

Beneath all of these travails, Roy is a pleasant, caring person. He rarely if ever raises his voice to his wife. There has never been any semblance of threat or intimidation, but it was clear that this was a family in distress. Roy's attention deficits were basic to this dysfunctional family. He was disorganized, inconsistent, and had memory problems, but like many overactive people could be socially outgoing while being insensitive to others.

What Roy and Carol had going for them was a commitment to the marriage. A multifocused treatment plan was provided to enable the family to begin the journey to becoming functional that included not only medication management, but also a practical plan to complete the construction tasks, partly through hiring additional help.

Roy and Carol took out a small second mortgage to pay for the extra help and for additional supplies to make their home livable. Each evening, Carol records on a small recording device (a "Voice-It"; see ADD WareHouse in the Appendix) a list of things that Roy has to do the next day. He carried the device in his shirt pocket and replayed it several times a day. In addition, an alphanumeric pager was provided by his employer, which he used to update and remind him of any tasks added during the day, including domestic tasks such as picking up the boys at the dentist.

WORK SITUATIONS

Adult ADHD symptoms are largely manifested at work, just as children's ADHD behaviors draw the most attention at school. Many adults with ADHD are either referred to or voluntarily see a clinician because of work-related problems. In evaluating an individual voicing ongoing work-related problems, clinicians should review thoroughly five general problem areas for signs of ADHD.

First, is the individual experiencing ongoing difficulties with getting paperwork done? Adults with ADHD are often regularly cited for procrastination in submitting reports, documentation, and expense account information. Second, does the individual have problems with long-term projects? Adults with ADHD have difficulty with planning and organizing, which manifests as missed project deadlines. Third, can the individual function well in a noisy work environment? Open modular offices without doors are impediments to an employee with ADHD, who needs a distraction-free environment with low ambient noise. Fourth, how much attention to detail does the individual's job require? Adults with ADHD seem better able at grasping the whole picture of the job but are less able at understanding the component details that go into making the big picture. Fifth, what percentage of the individual's work day is spent doing repetitive tasks? People with ADHD are ill suited for jobs that involve doing the same thing over and over. Certainly, all of us may have problems with these five areas, but the typical adult with ADHD is likely to have problems with all of them. These problems can be crippling in the workplace.

Most people would prefer to work in an environment with a minimum of distractions, but work conditions are far from ideal, and we learn to adapt. The difference between the worker with ADHD and the worker without is in the ability to screen out irrelevant noise. Adults with ADHD are distracted by it.

People with ADHD who receive no treatment or guidance do not seem to learn from their previous work experiences. Bright and capable men and women with ADHD may be unable to maintain long-term employment with a company. They often switch jobs, but because they do not fully understand the basis for their behaviors and frustrations, they usually end up in similar unsatisfying job situations. Frequently, such individuals will attempt to go into business for themselves as a way of controlling their work environment and work hours. But, being unaware of their ADHD and receiving no guidance, they once again experience similar problems with long-term projects and paperwork, resulting in business endeavors that flounder or fail.

In general, there is no occupation or profession that is "closed" to an adult with ADHD. The inattentiveness, impulsivity, hyperactivity, or distraction do not manifest themselves all of the time. In addition, adults with ADHD have other personality strengths and abilities that balance behavioral deficits and enable them to function in varying degrees of adequacy. In fact, many adults go through life not knowing that they have ADHD. However, when an individual comes into the clinician's office on his or her own volition or through an EAP referral on account of continuing work problems, significant stress, and a general inability to cope, ADHD symptoms can be diagnosed and the individual given timely help.

Case Vignette: Bob

An EAP manager sent Bob, age 26, a municipal employee, for consultation. The manager was bewildered, like Bob's immediate supervisor, by an apparent change in Bob's work ethic. Bob did well as a city planner for 5 years; he was then selected for promotion and given responsibility not only for his own projects but also for supervising three other entry-level city planners. This is when the difficulty began.

Bob lost the quietness of his own office and had to tend to the needs of other employees. He could no longer meet project deadlines. He became anxious, dysphoric, and irritable at home. His job performance deteriorated, and his family life also suffered. Bob was simply unable to do his work and supervise others at the same time. He was referred for job-related stress and treated for ADHD.

Case Vignette: Eileen

Eileen, age 52, works for a large corporation. She performed well on a variety of jobs and became a manager. After a time, she was transferred, as was the custom of the company, and thus reported to a new regional manager. Her new supervisor was "all business" and could not tolerate what Eileen described as her "occupational peculiarities."

The new office was divided into cubicles, so Eileen asked her manager if she could use a vacant storage room as her office. The manager refused, saying that it had no window. Eileen indicated that it was fine with her, because what she needed was to be away from noise of the office. The manager still refused because the new office could be perceived as preferential treatment.

Eileen had recognized earlier that she was more productive if she came in an hour or so before anyone else. This was an hour of quiet, with no office chatter or movement. Coming in early was therefore an attempt to self-treat her problems of coping with noise and distraction and was highly successful. Her new supervisor stopped this practice, however, even though it had caused no difficulties with her productivity or with her coworkers. He stated that he needed to treat all employees the same.

The restrictions that her supervisor placed on her caused her work product to deteriorate and produced increased anxiety, insomnia, and weight loss. Diagnosing and treating her ADHD and providing reasonable workplace accommodations put Eileen back on track. As mandated by the Americans with Disabilities Act of 1990, Eileen was permitted to come in early and allowed to use a headset with white noise to drown out distractions. Verbal instructions to her were replaced by instructions by memo or e-mail.

Case Vignette: Louise

Louise, age 25, is a first-grade teacher who had received very strong job reviews since she started in the school system 3 years previously. Because of these reviews, she was selected for a coveted position in an open-classroom environment. In this setting, two teachers shared a room two to three times the size of the normal classroom, with several "learning centers" for approximately 45 children.

Louise found it a difficult environment. She no longer controlled the classroom by herself but had to share authority. The classroom was less structured and organized. She had to deal with the children's initial unfamiliarity with the open-room environment. Louise began experiencing mild anxiety and panic attacks and began calling in sick when she felt that she could not face the "chaotic" classroom.

On the verge of losing her job, Louise began psychotherapy with little success. Further evaluation was requested. Louise was found to consume a considerable amount of energy controlling her ADHD symptomatology by becoming very organized. She made lists, made her lesson plans well in advance, and used a small recording device to dictate tasks. Many of these strategies could not be used in a large open classroom. The open environment was simply more than she could handle.

Louise requested and was granted a lateral transfer back to a standard first-grade environment. Having accomplished this transfer in a very short time, Louise declined any further treatment.

Case Vignette: Corbin

Corbin, age 62 and the father of two grown children, came in with his wife, who was convinced from a recent television segment on ADHD that Corbin had this problem. Corbin's history revealed that he had been married for 35 years, and in that time he had held 30 different jobs.

His inflexible thinking would get him into trouble. When a foreman on a construction site once asked him to stop putting up sheet rock in one room and to begin putting it up in another, Corbin could not make the shift. He was adamant about finishing the room he was in first, became verbally abusive, and was fired on the spot. On the other hand, Corbin was also known to walk off a job because it was too boring. He would quit impulsively for no reason. Corbin always found other employment, although not necessarily at a level consistent with his abilities. Keeping a job was another matter.

Twice before, Corbin's wife had convinced him to seek help. Records revealed that he was diagnosed with intermittent explosive personality disorder and "masked" depression. However, there was no documented evidence of explosive episodes or depressed symptomatology over time. A new evaluation found ADHD, including impulsivity, mood irritability, poor stress management, and inattention. Corbin expressed a willingness to change. He said that he did not take medicine even for a headache but would do so if it would help him keep a job.

The therapist had intermittent contact with Corbin for almost 4 years. He took his medication on work days and by the end of that time had held the same job for more than 3 years. He was looking forward to retirement at age 70. Working in the same place took the pressure off him. After 4 years his concerns were about seeking a change in jobs that would bring him closer to home, his wife's pending retirement, his need to continue working, and the sudden death of his oldest son.

THE MILITARY

The military has historically been viewed as a positive career choice for young adults with ADHD. The strict organization and scheduling of military personnel would appear to be an ideal environment; the person's job and attire are defined; and meals, housing, and health care are all provided and paid for by the government. Thus, the military lifestyle with clear rules, tasks, boundaries, structure, and organization attracts many adults with ADHD.

However, although parents and guardians may think that the military may be the best solution for solving a young adult's behavioral problems, there are times in which this is an inappropriate choice. Military life and "top-down" organizational structure can be problematic for adults with ADHD. Following orders and out-of-focus impulsivity and disorganized behavior can be antithetical to the military code of justice and chain-of-command decision making. Early discharge for the "good of the service" or worse, a court-martial, can result.

It is the general policy of the U.S. Armed Services that men and women receiving pharmacological management for ADHD cannot be inducted into the military. An individual with a history of ADHD should be off medications for at least 1 year prior to the induction. However, this standard duration may be lowered, depending on the needs of the military and its ability to meet recruiting goals. Being off pharmacological treatment does not ensure induction into the military if otherwise qualified; recruiters take the best from their pool of applicants.

It is less clear what happens to enlisted personnel who, while in the military, are identified as having ADHD. The diagnosis often comes to light either through self-disclosure of one's problems or the immediate supervisor's request for a clinical evaluation because of mission-related behavioral difficulties. The most likely outcome for the enlisted individual is an honorable discharge with no loss of benefits. On occasion, depending on the needs of the military, a person may be transferred from a combat or supportive military post to an administrative post away from combat operations.

To my knowledge, there is no specific policy in the military toward enlisted persons found to have or admit to having ADHD. However, informal conversations with military recruiters lead me to believe that if a person in the military were confirmed to have ADHD, the person would likely be discharged from active duty. The military's concern about not recruiting adults known to have ADHD is based on its prime objective: maintenance of combat readiness. The individual with ADHD could jeopardize or compromise a military mission, as the increased stress of combat could aggravate symptoms.

Most adults with ADHD who make it into the military generally have undistinguished military careers. But most do a creditable job of serving their country. In some cases, adults with ADHD in the military have demonstrated considerable courage and outstanding performance. General George Patton, a World War II hero, was believed to have had ADHD, but the diagnosis did not exist during his time.

On completing their term of enlistment, most servicemen and women are usually discharged honorably with neither they nor the military establishment aware of an ADHD condition. They may even have received the Good Conduct Medal, an award given to enlisted men and women for 3 years of "exemplary military behavior." Clinicians should check for possible ADHD in an adult who was discharged early under a "quality retention" program. Servicemen and women who are discharged under this program are generally reported as having performed their duties well and may even have been decorated, but a problem was noted with some part of their training, job performance, or physical fitness.

Case Vignette: Larry

Larry, age 22 and a high school graduate, was recently discharged from the army. After completing basic training and advanced infantry training, he was stationed in Germany. Larry, a low-energy individual, had some minor problems getting through the physical training in boot camp. He received an expert rating on the M-16 rifle, the grenade launcher, and the .45-calibre pistol.

Both in Germany and on his return to the United States, his sergeants had raised concern about his increasing weight, which was close to the upper limit of the acceptable range. Larry was counseled by his sergeant to lose weight. The military approach to counseling was simple: Losing weight was in his best interest because he was a combat soldier and, for the good of the service and its mission, he should be in form to fight for his country. Larry was given an order to lose weight, with no setting of intermediate goals and no monitoring of his progress. After several months, no weight loss was evident, and the same sergeant issued the same set of instructions.

Larry had considered making the military a career because he enjoyed his work and had been decorated for outstanding service. Unfortunately, on very short notice, he was told that he was being discharged under the quality retention program because his weight had crossed over the line. Larry's ADHD got in the way of his planning and organization. He had bought diet food and drinks by the case, but without someone to set up short-term goals and monitor progress, he was unable to succeed in losing weight.

Larry illustrates another important issue. On a mission, he functioned well, with no problem with concentration, attention, and job performance. But out of harm's way, at his duty station in Germany between missions, he could not lose weight on his own. His disorganization evidenced itself at discharge, when he could not find certain pieces of equipment or clothing that had to be returned to the army.

RECREATION AND LEISURE

What an adult does for leisure and recreation could be a possible indicator of ADHD symptoms. As mentioned earlier, individuals who get pleasure from high-risk activities, such as skydiving, bungee jumping, or gambling, may have ADHD. A significant point that clinicians should be sensitive to is when the individual complains of no longer enjoying recreation or leisure time because he or she has difficulty concentrating or paying attention to recreational activities.

Conclusion

In most clinical evaluations, ADHD is an important diagnosis to determine. The clinical evaluation should consider problems in every aspect of the individual's life, recognizing that ADHD problems may not manifest themselves in all areas of a person's functioning but may show up in more than one aspect of behavior. Clinicians should be mindful of how this disorder masquerades and simulates other disorders and also should be mindful of comorbidities such as depression. This may be particularly important when making a primary diagnosis other than ADHD and treatment is provided. Some improvement will be noted following the treatment, but significant problems may still persist in areas outside of the boundaries of the primary diagnosis. In such instances, the clinician would do well to consider the possibility of an additional diagnosis of ADHD.

References and Resources

Barkley, R. A. (1998). *Attention-deficit-hyperactivity disorder: A handbook for diagnosis and treatment* (2nd ed.). New York: Guilford Press.

Cook, J. (1997). *The book of positive quotations.* Minneapolis, MN: Fairview Press.

Murphy, K., & Barkley, R. A. (1996). Attention deficit hyperactivity disorder in adults. *Comprehensive Psychiatry, 37,* 393–401.

Nadeau, K. G. (1996). *Adventures in fast forward: Life, love, and work for the ADD adult.* New York: Brunner-Mazel.

Weiss, M., Hechtman, L. T., & Weiss, G. (1999). *ADHD in adulthood: A guide to current theory, diagnosis, and treatment.* Baltimore: Johns Hopkins University Press.

Wender, P. H. (1995). *Attention-deficit-hyperactivity disorders in adulthood.* New York: Oxford University Press.

Diagnostic Criteria, Differential Diagnosis, and Comorbidity | 4

No matter how far you have gone on a wrong road, turn back.
—Turkish proverb

ADHD can stand alone, present like another disorder such as anxiety, or be comorbid with another disorder such as depression. Making the correct diagnosis is always a challenge. This chapter discusses the diagnostic criteria for adult ADHD, differential diagnoses, and comorbid disorders. Problems associated with ADHD not being diagnosed in childhood will also be discussed to aid clinicians in understanding the adult presentation.

The Missed Diagnosis

Adults who have ADHD should have observable, reportable, or verifiable (through testing) symptoms in one or more of the four core symptom areas of functioning as early as in childhood: inattention, distractibility, impulsivity, and (sometimes) hyperactivity. Hyperactivity may run the continuum from, for example, the seated individual who is restless and fidgety to the individual who prefers not to sit but rather wanders around the room.

There are several factors that can mitigate against childhood diagnosis of ADHD. Conduct and academic problems frequently trigger parent–teacher conferences, evaluation, and testing. However, home and school environments vary in their tolerance levels for the whole range of ADHD behaviors, such that certain behavior may never reach the threshold for intervention. For example, children with ADHD with high intelligence may be overlooked because their IQs permit good academic performance and may make their ADHD symptoms and behaviors more acceptable. On the other end of the continuum, the nonhyperactive child with ADHD is less likely to be selected for evaluation and treatment. In addition, girls with significant attention problems frequently are not diagnosed because they generally do not misbehave in school. However, even in homes and schools that are highly structured and supportive, many children with attention deficits will still remain undiagnosed and untreated.

Most people with attention deficits do not "outgrow it." Most adults with ADHD seeking treatment today were not diagnosed as children, and they have suffered varying degrees of problems for decades. Strict adherence to the requirement of clear evidence of symptoms in childhood has prevented some hyperactive adults with ADHD and many nonhyperactive adults from obtaining proper diagnosis and treatment. The ADD/ADHD nomenclature became "official" in 1980 (*DSM-III*); by that time, many of today's adults had already finished high school. Clinicians should keep in mind that rigid interpretation of *DSM-IV* ADHD criteria is not sufficient for properly assessing and diagnosing adults with ADHD.

Case Vignette: Harold

Harold, age 35, came in for evaluation for what he believed to be ADHD. He was college educated and had read many popular publications about ADHD and decided that he had every symptom. In the course of the diagnostic interview, Harold indicated that he could go for several days with little sleep. In addition, he would make multiple lists of things to do without accomplishing any of them. He stated that he could go on this way for many days and that his "hyperactivity" would diminish but his concentration and impulsivity continued. His disorganization continued as well. Harold was adamant about starting pharmacological treatment with Ritalin to control ADHD.

His primary care physician was unclear about the diagnosis and requested a consultation. Harold's inattention, elevated activity, and problems in concentration looked at first like ADHD. In fact, his core problem was not ADHD but unipolar disorder, manic type. Mood stabilizers and psychotherapy were very effective.

Diagnostic Criteria

As discussed in chapter 1, the definitions of ADHD, as well as the recommended criteria for determining a diagnosis, have varied considerably throughout the history of this disorder. ADHD in adulthood is now medically recognized as a mental disorder, and it is endorsed by and included in the *DSM-IV* (American Psychiatric Association, 1994). A variety of terms have been used for ADHD. Some prefer ADD to emphasize the attention aspect of the disorder rather than the hyperactivity component (which is not universal and may diminish in adulthood). I use ADHD to cover all three types—inattentive, hyperactive–impulsive, or combined.

Currently, the primary characteristics of ADHD and the diagnostic criteria in clinical use in the United States are outlined in the *DSM-IV.* It is similar, although not identical, to the definition in the *ICD-10* (WHO, 1992) used in Europe. The *DSM-IV* criteria are a considerable improvement over those provided in the earlier versions of the *DSM* (Barkley, 1998).

The *DSM-III, DSM-III-R,* and *DSM-IV* all agree that the core symptoms consist of an inattention domain and a hyperactivity–impulsivity domain (Cantwell, 1996). *DSM-IV* lists these core symptoms as the 2 core dimensions of the disorder, with 9 symptoms under each dimension (see Exhibit 4.1). Barkley (1998) pointed out that the requirement of impairment as a criterion for diagnosis of a mental disorder in general and ADHD in particular is crucial. A child or an adult who demonstrates a high frequency (or severity) of ADHD-related symptoms does not necessarily have ADHD. Rather, only when the severity of an individual's ADHD-related symptoms interferes with or disrupts one or more of the individual's major life activities—at home, school, or work—can a diagnosis of ADHD or other mental disorder be made.

There is general agreement that ADHD in adulthood is a continuation of various symptoms in childhood and, therefore, ADHD is similar in both groups. However, researchers and practitioners also have noted that although the *DSM-IV* diagnostic criteria was devised for both children and adults, the criteria have not been entirely useful in the diagnosis of adult ADHD. Field trials are needed on adults with ADHD.

Issues continue to be raised on whether the "cutoff point" for diagnosis should be the same for adults and children. Some argue that the cutoff should be lower for adults, who may be disabled by some symptoms but have developed coping skills to deal with others; norms may be less clear for adults than for children such that the degree of impairment associated with a symptom may be difficult to evaluate (Weiss, Hechtman, & Weiss, 1999, p. 8). Some of the major clinical complaints expressed by adults with ADHD are not listed in the *DSM-IV,* such as procrastination, a chronic sense of failure, involvement in too many things simultaneously and completion of none, and poor time management. This shortcoming has prompted the development of other diagnostic criteria for ADHD in adults, such as that developed by Hallowell

EXHIBIT 4.1

DSM-IV Criteria for ADHD

A. Either (1) or (2):
   (1) Six (or more) of the following symptoms of *inattention* have persisted for at least 6 months to a degree that is maladaptive and inconsistent with developmental level:
   Inattention
   (a) often fails to give close attention to details or makes careless mistakes in schoolwork, work, or other activities
   (b) often has difficulty sustaining attention in tasks or play activities
   (c) often does not seem to listen when spoken to directly
   (d) often does not follow through on instructions and fails to finish schoolwork, chores, or duties in the workplace (not due to oppositional behavior or failure to understand instructions)
   (e) often has difficulty organizing tasks and activities
   (f) often avoids, dislikes, or is reluctant to engage in tasks that require sustained mental effort (such as schoolwork or homework)
   (g) often loses things necessary for tasks or activities (e.g., toys, school assignments, pencils, books, or tools)
   (h) is often easily distracted by extraneous stimuli
   (i) is often forgetful in daily activities
   (2) Six (or more) of the following symptoms of *hyperactivity–impulsivity* have persisted for at least 6 months to a degree that is maladaptive and inconsistent with developmental level:
   Hyperactivity
   (a) often fidgets with hands or feet or squirms in seat
   (b) often leaves seat in classroom or in other situations in which remaining seated is expected
   (c) often runs about or climbs excessively in situations in which it is inappropriate (in adolescents or adults, may be limited to subjective feelings of restlessness)
   (d) often has difficulty playing or engaging in leisure activities quietly
   (e) is often "on the go" or often acts as if "driven by a motor"
   (f) often talks excessively
   Impulsivity
   (g) often blurts out answers before the questions have been completed
   (h) often has difficulty awaiting turn
   (i) often interrupts or intrudes on others (e.g., butts into conversations or games)
B. Some hyperactive–impulsive or inattentive symptoms that caused impairment were present before age 7 years.
C. Some impairment from the symptoms is present in two or more settings (e.g., at school [or work] and at home).
D. There must be clear evidence of clinically significant impairment in social, academic, or occupational functioning.
E. The symptoms do not occur exclusively during the course of a Pervasive Developmental Disorder, Schizophrenia, or other Psychotic Disorder and are not better accounted for by another mental disorder (e.g., Mood Disorder, Anxiety Disorder, Dissociative Disorder, or a Personality Disorder).

(continued)

EXHIBIT 4.1 continued

Code based on type:
314.01   Attention-Deficit/Hyperactivity Disorder, Combined Type: if both Criteria A1 and A2 are met for the past 6 months.
314.00   Attention-Deficit/Hyperactivity Disorder, Predominantly Inattentive Type: if Criterion A1 is met, but Criterion A2 is not met for the past 6 months.
314.01   Attention-Deficit/Hyperactivity Disorder, Predominantly Hyperactive–Impulsive Type: if Criterion A2 is met, but Criterion A1 is not met for the past 6 months.
Coding note: For individuals (especially adolescents and adults) who currently have symptoms that no longer meet full criteria, "In Partial Remission" should be specified.

Note. From *Diagnostic and Statistical Manual of Mental Disorders* (4th ed., pp. 83–85), by the American Psychiatric Association, 1994, Washington, DC: Author. Copyright 1994 by the American Psychiatric Association. Reprinted with permission.

and Ratey (1994; see Exhibit 4.2) and Wender (1995; see Exhibit 4.3). Wender's Utah Criteria for Adult ADD were the first diagnostic system to be developed for adult ADHD. The criteria were the basis for much research and clinical diagnosis in the field, and they have been widely used by practitioners and researchers (Weiss et al., 1999).

The Hallowell and Ratey (1994) criteria were developed based on their clinical experience and emphasize the full range of symptoms associated with adult ADHD. Weiss et al. (1999) pointed out that the Hallowell and Ratey criteria include some types of behavior that the *DSM-IV* would list under "Associated Features." They also include some behaviors that might be better listed under "Coexisting Disorders," such as substance abuse. Wender's (1995) Utah criteria focuses on the core symptoms of adult ADHD without going into associated symptoms or findings, such as substance abuse or family history. The Hallowell and Ratey criteria have many points in common with the Wender criteria.

The two diagnostic criteria differ mainly in that the Hallowell and Ratey (1994) criteria include a syndrome of ADHD without hyperactivity, whereas Wender (1995) does not. Wender himself recognized that ADHD without hyperactivity exists as a clinical syndrome, but he chose not to include it in his Utah criteria because the criteria were developed primarily for research purposes (and Wender used a homogeneous set of patients by excluding those without a history of hyperactivity). Hallowell and Ratey argued that in their clinical experience, they have seen many individuals, particularly women, who present with ADHD symptoms under both sets of criteria, except that they do not have a history of hyperactivity. These patients' symptoms cannot be explained by any condition other than ADHD, and they do not respond well to any medical treatment other than the treatment for ADHD. For these reasons, Hallowell and Ratey chose to include these nonhyperactive patients as meeting their diagnostic criteria for adult ADHD (pp. 76–77).

EXHIBIT 4.2

Hallowell and Ratey's (1994) Diagnostic Criteria for ADD in Adults

A. Chronic disturbance in which at least 15 of the following are present:
   1. a sense of underachievement, of not meeting one's goals (regardless of how much one has actually accomplished)
   2. difficulty in getting organized
   3. chronic procrastination or trouble getting started
   4. many projects going simultaneously; trouble with follow-through
   5. tendency to say what comes to mind without necessarily considering the timing or appropriateness of the remark
   6. a frequent search for high stimulation
   7. an intolerance of boredom
   8. easy distractibility, trouble focusing attention, tendency to tune out or drift away in the middle of a page or a conversation, often coupled with an ability to hyperfocus at times
   9. often creative, intuitive, highly intelligent
   10. trouble in going through established channels, following "proper" procedure
   11. impatient; low tolerance for frustration
   12. impulsive, either verbally or in action, as in impulsive spending of money, changing plans, enacting new schemes or career plans, and the like
   13. tendency to worry needlessly, endlessly; tendency to scan the horizon looking for something to worry about, alternating with inattention to or disregard for actual dangers
   14. sense of insecurity
   15. mood swings, mood lability, especially when disengaged from a person or a project (These mood swings are not as pronounced as those associated with manic–depressive illness or depression.)
   16. restlessness (Not the full-blown hyperactivity usually seen in a child, but more like "nervous energy": pacing, drumming fingers, shifting position while sitting, leaving a table or room frequently, feeling edgy while at rest.)
   17. tendency toward addictive behavior (The addiction may be to a substance such as alcohol or cocaine, or to an activity, such as gambling, shopping, eating, or overwork.)
   18. chronic problems with self-esteem
   19. inaccurate self-observation
   20. family history of ADD or manic–depressive illness or depression or substance abuse or other disorders of impulse control or mood
B. Childhood history of ADD (It may not have been formally diagnosed, but in reviewing the history, the signs and symptoms are there.)
C. Situation not explained by other medical or psychiatric condition.

Note. Consider a criterion met only if the behavior is considerably more frequent than that of most people of the same mental age. From *Driven to Distraction* (pp. 73–76), by E. M. Hallowell and J. J. Ratey, 1994, New York: Pantheon Books. Copyright 1994 by Pantheon Books. Adapted with permission.

EXHIBIT 4.3

Utah Criteria for ADHD in Adults

Part I. Child Characteristics
   A childhood history consistent with ADHD in childhood as defined by A or B.
A. *Narrow criteria:* The individual met *DSM-III-R* criteria for ADHD in childhood (8 of the 13 symptoms or signs).
B. *Broad criteria:* Both characteristics 1 and 2, and one characteristic from 3–6.
   1. Hyperactivity. More active than other children, unable to sit still, fidgety, restless, always on the go, talking excessively.
   2. Attention deficits, sometimes described as a "short attention span," distractibility, daydreaming, failure to finish assignments in class or complete homework, was called lazy, was said not to remember, was told could do better than did. Underachievement not due primarily to learning disorders (dyslexia) or to deficits in intelligence.
   3. Behavior problems in school. Talking in class, disciplined more than classmates, called out for disrupting the class, stayed after school. Disciplined by teachers, principal.
   4. Impulsivity. Could not wait for turn, acted without thinking, blurted things out, got into accidents, reckless.
   5. Overexcitability or temper outbursts, got into many fights.
   6. Temper outbursts.

Part II. Adult Characteristics
A. The presence in adulthood of (1) motor hyperactivity and (2) attention deficits, together with at least two of characteristics 3–7.
   1. Persistent motor hyperactivity.
   2. Attention deficits, impaired concentration, distractibility.
   3. Affective lability.
   4. Hot temper: explosive, short-lived outbursts, transient loss of control, easily provoked or constant irritability, impatience.
   5. Disorganization and inability to complete tasks.
   6. Stress intolerance.
   7. Impulsivity.
B. Absence of the following symptoms:
   1. Bipolar and depressive mood disorders.
   2. Schizophrenia, schizoaffective disorder, schizotypal personality disorder; the woolly (vague, meandering) thinking (speech) of schizophrenic spectrum disorder.
   3. Borderline personality disorder:
      a. A pattern of unstable and intense interpersonal relationships, characterized by alternating between extremes of overidealization and devaluation.
      b. Recurrent suicide threats, gestures, or behavior, or any self-mutilating behavior.
      c. Prominent identity disturbances.
      d. Pronounced and chronic feelings of emptiness.
      e. Frantic efforts to avoid real or imagined abandonment and intolerance of being alone.
   4. Antisocial personality disorder, alcohol or drug abuse within the past year, or any history of stimulant drug abuse.

Note. From *Attention-Deficit-Hyperactivity Disorders in Adults* (pp. 241–243) by P. H. Wender, 1995, New York: Oxford University Press and from *ADHD in Adulthood: A Guide to Current Theory, Diagnosis, and Treatment* (pp. 15–17), by M. Weiss, L. T. Hechtman, & G. Weiss, 1999, Baltimore: Johns Hopkins University Press.

Differential Diagnosis and Comorbidity

In differential diagnosis of ADHD, there are conditions that in some cases may be comorbid and in other cases may mimic ADHD. Absence seizures, for instance, may mimic the clinical presence of ADHD in some cases and may be associated with a "true" ADHD syndrome in others. The clinician must be able to rule out the presence of other behavioral, developmental, medical, and neurological disorders and determine whether these are comorbid or whether they are mimicking ADHD (Cantwell, 1996).

The clinician's task of assessing patients for differential diagnosis can be daunting and challenging, controversial, and time consuming. Some disorders that are comorbid with ADHD present primarily in childhood, whereas others surface primarily in adulthood. Some comorbid disorders may be the consequence of or related to the ADHD and may show significant amelioration when the ADHD is aggressively treated, for example, antisocial behavior, depression, and anxiety. The clinician with expertise in childhood disorders may be unfamiliar with the residual problems that could carry over to adulthood; conversely, the clinician treating adults may be unfamiliar with childhood disorders. In addition, a number of symptoms not required for a diagnosis of ADHD in the *DSM-IV* are commonly associated with ADHD in adults: procrastination, low tolerance of frustration, mood lability and a sense of failure, low self-esteem, and impairment of social skills (Weiss et al., 1999).

DEPRESSION

Depression is the most common comorbid finding in clinical practice, and it is a frequent finding in the families of individuals with ADHD. Estimates are that up to 44% of children with ADHD may have at least one other psychiatric disorder, 32% have two other disorders, and 11% have at least three other disorders (Szatmari, Offord, & Boyle, 1989). Several studies have shown ratings of children with ADHD as having more symptoms of anxiety, depression or dysthymia, and low self-esteem than do normal children or children with learning disabilities who do not have ADHD (e.g., Biederman, Faraone, Mick, Moore, & Lelon, 1996; Bohline, 1985; Breen & Barkley, 1983, 1984; J. B. Jensen, Burke, & Garfinkel, 1988).

What may not be clear is how much of these mood spectrum problems in adults with ADHD are comorbid and how much are actually the sadness, futility, and "giving up" resulting from having lived with undiagnosed attention deficits for many years. It is difficult, and sometimes even impossible, to clearly discriminate an adult with ADHD, primarily inattentive type, from an individual who presents with depression. Individuals with dysthymia or low-grade major depressive episodes without psychotic symptoms or suicidal behavior can present a difficult diagnostic dilemma, and comorbid ADHD may not be diagnosable immediately. However, it should be kept in mind. Furthermore, there are adults with attention deficits who have an anhedonic quality to their personality and behavior. They experience no pleasure or excitement around things that would ordinarily engender pleasure or happiness to most people, such as birthdays, anniversaries, and successes. Depression in ADHD disorders is more cyclical, in which the individual swings from excitement to depression in a matter of minutes or hours, when compared to mood disorders lasting weeks and months.

Case Vignette: Ann Marie

Ann Marie, age 33, is a high school graduate who is married and has a 12-year-old daughter. She is a clerk-typist for the state government. She came in for evaluation on referral from her primary care physician.

Ann Marie had completed a 10-item questionnaire that was being passed around her office, and after scoring "positive" for ADHD, she went to her physician asking for Ritalin. She did have long-standing problems. She complained of low energy and sadness lasting weeks at a time, although she had never been suicidal. She had had problems falling asleep and waking too early in the morning. One of her aunts had been treated for depression.

Ann Marie rated her situation as relatively bad—4 on a scale of 1–10, where 1 is *as bad as things can get,* and 10 is *as good as things can get.* When asked what would improve her self-rating, she said having more energy and getting more work done. She did not consider herself depressed, just sad. She went on to describe problems with concentration and inattention. Computerized assessment found these problems to be significant, although these procedures cannot discriminate between ADHD- and depression-based inattention. Rating scales were suggestive of ADHD but not significantly so.

Her husband considered her a good mother and wife and had not noticed anything of concern. In passing, however, he said that it would be good if Ann Marie could get things done sooner, referring to household chores such as preparing dinner and washing clothes.

In collaboration with the primary care physician, Ann Marie was started on an antidepressant, as depression seemed to be the primary diagnosis, with a possible comorbid finding of ADHD. When she returned with her husband after having reached maintenance level on the antidepressants, her earlier sad expression had disappeared. She had more energy and slept better. However, she still daydreamed often, and her work had not improved that much.

Inattention and daydreaming at work seemed to be facilitated by the environment. With the cooperation of her section chief, she changed her cubicle to one in a corner with no windows to reduce distractions and noise. At home, she began to use self-adhesive notes to keep a shopping list on the refrigerator. Her husband noted some improvement. Further follow-up did not occur, as Ann Marie called to say that everything was fine and that she did not need to come in again.

Case Vignette: Gladys

Gladys, age 21, is a college senior who had been on the verge of failing college since her freshman year. Her low grade point average kept her on the edge of being asked to withdraw. She was regularly required to attend summer school to increase her average. As typical for many adults with attention problems, she found a summer school course to be a positive academic environment. The focus on a single content area over a relatively short period of time better supported her concentration. She did not have to make mental shifts between courses or to adapt to different instructional styles.

Gladys appeared to be a pleasant and sociable person, as her parents and her college advisor confirmed. However, as far as anyone could remember, she never got excited or upset about grades, dating, going to college, or attending summer school. Her parents indicated how surprised they had been about her lack of excitement about birthdays and parties ever since childhood. As with many patients with ADHD, her anhedonic reactions reduced the efficacy of the usual rewards and consequences used to motivate children.

ANXIETY

Reviews of literature estimate that the overlap of ADHD with anxiety disorders range between 10% to 40%, suggesting that, on average, about 25% of children with ADHD were likely to have such a disorder (Biederman, Newcorn, & Sprich, 1991). The comorbidity of anxiety or mood disorder along with ADHD is associated with a history of greater family and personal stress, greater parental symptoms of anxiety and mood disturbance, and reduced responsiveness to stimulant medication (P. S. Jensen, Martin, & Cantwell, 1997).

Because anxiety can cause significant interruption in attention, concentration, and memory (presenting as forgetfulness) in an adult with these symptoms, the clinician should take care to rule out this in the

ADHD diagnosis. Panic and phobic disorders have not been often associated with ADHD, although they can exist. In general, individuals with a principal diagnosis of generalized anxiety disorder will show signs of anxiety across most situations and with inattention and loss of concentration during episodes of significantly increased anxiety. Because many adults with ADHD have an intolerance for everyday stress, their inability to cope with stress may present as anxiety. A careful history of the patient's behavior during the school age years in relation to the ADHD core symptom cluster can help clarify the diagnostic picture.

Case Vignette: Katey

Katey, age 31, is a successful real estate agent. Her chief complaint was difficulty with concentration and a constant worry that she might forget some detail of a real estate closing, which has happened on occasion. Her anxiety caused problems on the job and interfered with her sleep. She described herself as becoming more stressed and preoccupied with these difficulties. Her poor concentration and forgetfulness suggested an inattentive ADHD.

As a child, Katey was described by teachers as usually very sociable but on other occasions as a "space cadet" who did not know where the rest of the class was in its daily lessons. Diagnostic questionnaires and computerized assessment indicated ADHD. Psychological treatment to help her understand the nature and behavioral expression of her ADHD brought significant improvement and reduced her feeling of stress. She was opposed to any pharmocotherapy. She was still somewhat anxious, and the therapist continued treatment, now with a primary diagnosis of generalized anxiety disorder with secondary ADHD.

In helping Katey deal with her ADHD, the therapist focused on modifying behavior. She was concerned that she might forget some aspect of a real estate closing due to inattention. She began using a Franklin Planner, a system that allows not for appointments and schedules but for a listing of tasks that can be carried forward if not completed. This kept her better focused without increasing her stress. Her computer skills were used to build two documents: a chart that showed what needed to be done at a closing and templates of various forms, both assembled in a computerized file that could be copied for each client.

OBSESSIVE–COMPULSIVE AND PANIC DISORDERS

Obsessive–compulsive disorders are easy to discriminate from ADHD, and they do not appear to be significantly related to ADHD. However, obsessive–compulsive personality traits may be observed in adults with ADHD. Generally, adults with ADHD with obsessive–compulsive traits may involve a level of preoccupation or overfocusing to the detriment of a larger task or goal. Often such attempts at "perfectionism" are a compensatory strategy for a disorganized and unstructured existence. However, the underlying anxiety driving obsessive–compulsive behavior is absent in individuals who are compensating for their ADHD. This presentation does not suggest ADHD. Ritualistic, repetitive, irrational patterns of behavior are absent in ADHD. However, if the obsessive–compulsive symptoms are not driven by anxiety, but are instead attempts to stabilize a chaotic, disorganized environment, then ADHD is the more appropriate primary diagnosis.

Similarly, for panic disorders, the crucial issue is determining what may be causing the underlying anxiety. Anxiety may precipitate panic symptoms, both physiological and cognitive, followed by a full-blown panic attack. Further evaluation may suggest the possibility of some other disorder copresenting with panic disorder, but comorbid ADHD and panic disorder are almost unheard of.

ANTISOCIAL PERSONALITY

In children with ADHD, conduct disorder has a high comorbidity; among adults with ADHD, antisocial personality behaviors are also common. Some studies in both state and federal prisons suggest a very high incidence of ADHD among incarcerated populations.

People with antisocial personalities rarely seek professional care at their own initiative. When an evaluation is requested by an attorney or a judge, a careful evaluation for an ADHD precursor or comorbid condition should be completed. It is not a great leap behaviorally from being impulsive and overactive with cravings for excitement and risk taking, seen in an ADHD population, to breaking the law to release all of this energy.

Contrary to popular belief, ADHD-based antisocial behavior is amenable to treatment and improvement. Recent research from ADHD prison populations in Colorado, Washington, and California has shown that offenders who were educated about and treated for their ADHD had a significantly lower rate of recidivism than those who were not treated (K. Nadeau, personal communication, March 12, 2000). ADHD-based antisocial behavior is quite different from antisocial personality disorder. Individuals with ADHD know the rules, but they cannot put in place the appropriate behavioral safeguards to follow them. In marked contrast, individuals with antisocial personality disorder know the rules but simply choose not to follow them.

Case Vignette: Kenny

Kenny, a high school graduate in his mid-20s, has been paying three to five times the rate of his age mates for automobile insurance. He has had ongoing problems with speeding, having been charged several times with reckless driving (driving more than 20 miles an hour over the posted speed limit). Kenny reported being "just stupid"; he never thought about the speed limit while he drove.

I met Kenny when his lawyer, who had a history of ADHD herself, asked me to see her client. That took some coordination, because he was under house arrest with an ankle alarm. It was difficult to determine whether Kenny simply liked to speed, as he showed no remorse, or did not attend to speed limits because of inattention and distractibility. Speeding is typical of patients with ADHD and is often combined with poor judgment, impulsivity, and a lack of forethought or planning. Kenny gave no impression of trying to get away with speeding. He seemed to be genuinely perplexed by his behavior.

An ADHD evaluation, including computerized assessment, indicated ADHD, primarily the impulsive–hyperactive type. A combination of pharmacology and cognitive–behavior therapy was prescribed and helped modify his behavior. Kenny began to understand his behavior and realized that he was not "just stupid." His routines were restructured to reduce the incentive to speed. He began to get up earlier in the morning so as not to be rushed to get to work. Kenny laid out his clothes at night before going to bed and showered in the evening. He was encouraged to talk to his employer about last-minute assignments that required the use of his car. A slight change in office routine permitted Kenny to complete all of his assignments outside of the office by noon.

Case Vignette: Steven

Steven, age 17, received three speeding tickets over a period of 8 weeks. One of the tickets was also for reckless driving (defined as traveling 20 or more miles over the posted speed limit). Two of the three tickets were received while traveling the same two-mile section of the interstate.

After Steven's third ticket his father (this author) discussed his driving record with him. Steven concluded that his speeding tickets were not his fault. He stated that if we were not allowed to drive such a fast car, then he would not be receiving speeding tickets. I asked Steven to accompany me to the garage where the car was. I opened the driver's door, pointed to the accelerator, and asked Steven to identify it, which he did. I did the same with the brake and the clutch. I then pointed to another control and asked Steven what it was, and he said "that's the cruise control." I said simply, "Aha!"

BIPOLAR DISORDER

There can be "true" bipolar disorders that present with ADHD, or ADHD that is comorbid with the bipolar disorder. Indeed, about 10% of adults with ADHD are comorbid with bipolar disorder. During a patient's initial presentation, the mixture of mood irritability with boredom or feeling discontent and high energy level can be perplexing to a clinician. Hyperactivity and impulsivity can look very much like mania or hypomania. Likewise, individuals with bipolar disorder can be distractible and high-risk takers, just like adults with ADHD.

The two disorders share additional symptoms of irritable mood and stream-of-consciousness thinking (i.e., things moving so fast through one's mind that they blend together). Are cases with these symptoms ADHD, bipolar disorder, or both? Because ADHD is not an exclusionary diagnosis, it could be both. The differential diagnosis may be facilitated by a positive family history of bipolar disorder or a well-documented personal (and verifiable) history of mania. It would not be unusual to find that a person with ADHD has a relative with bipolar disorder.

In addition, the mania or manic episode must last for a week or more coupled with an elevated, irritable, or expansive mood. Mood shifts in ADHD are not cyclic and last for hours to days rather than weeks to months as in bipolar disorder. The irritability and affective lability of individuals with ADHD are generally caused by low frustration tolerance and some rigidity in thinking, and mood may change several times during a single day.

Sleeping patterns may differ: A person with a bipolar disorder may operate on little to no sleep and maintain expansive mood, whereas the individual with ADHD may have trouble sleeping because he or she is thinking about the past day's events or the next day's tasks. Pressured or driven speech is more likely to be associated with bipolar disorder. Last, "thought racing, "a stream of consciousness so rapid that it cannot be managed or slowed down, that is associated with bipolar disorders is decidedly different from the "thought overload" manifested in adults with ADHD, in which they must try to remember and sort through many thoughts and ideas to get anything done. ADHD is more pervasive than bipolar disorder, because the mood swings are more episodic. Psychotic features are not seen in ADHD.

Case Vignette: James

James, in his mid-40s, stated that he had ADHD, that his doctor had put him on Ritalin, and that everything was "perfect." His primary care physician just wanted confirmation of the diagnosis for his records. Neither he nor his physician was interested in any other treatment approach.

Although the computerized assessment showed evidence of inattention, the clinical interview was enlightening. James showed pressured speech and thought racing—not just having a lot of things to think about as some ADHD adults do. This raised a concern about the presence of a bipolar disorder. This was further supported when, after some time, James addressed the depressed side of his functioning. The therapist suggested that he should be evaluated for a mood stabilizer. Some children diagnosed and treated successfully for ADHD develop bipolar symptoms as young adults. Treatment must be serial, starting with the diagnosis causing the greater problems.

James was adamant that he wanted to stay on the Ritalin, although he was experiencing side effects such as euphoria and insomnia that were not simply part of a manic phase. The problem was not resolved until James finally agreed to allow the therapist to contact his primary care physician and was subsequently treated for his mania.

SUBSTANCE ABUSE

Practitioners who work with the substance-abusing population should always be mindful of a comorbid finding of ADHD. Studies have indicated that between 14% and 33% of substance abusers also can have a diagnosis of ADHD (e.g., Tzelepis, Schubinger, & Warbasse, 1995).

Drugs of choice among this group of individuals with ADHD are alcohol, opiates, and cocaine. Caffeine also may be consumed in large quantities in attempts at self-medication. These drugs reduce the pain of dysphoria, boredom, repeated failure, and "feeling bad because I don't know what's wrong with me."

There is considerable discussion in the ADHD literature that drug use and abuse may be a common outcome of undiagnosed ADHD (see Wender, 1995). This is not surprising when one considers that the person with ADHD can go in one of two directions. First, living with and receiving no treatment for the discomfort and frustration of ADHD-related problems can lead individuals to self-medicate. Conversely, individuals with ADHD may abuse drugs because of their impulsive and overactive behavior. If, in addition to being hyperactive and impulsive, they are also high-risk takers, they also are more vulnerable to trying substances and alcohol.

The pharmacological drug of choice for treating ADHD is methylphenidate HCL (Ritalin). Like cocaine, methylphenidate, when consumed by most people with ADHD, produces an experience of significantly greater focus but without a feeling of being high. This point is well made by an encounter with a 20-year-old man who abused several substances and who, when asked if he ever took "speed," said, "Hell, no! I did that once, and everybody else was high and having a great time while I sat watching a dumb movie on TV."

Comorbid ADHD and substance abuse have important treatment and outcome implications. For example, inpatient drug rehabilitation programs are usually configured in 7-day to 10-day experiences consisting of concentrated, day-long sessions, with some activities continuing well into the evenings. If individuals in drug rehabilitation programs are undiagnosed and untreated for ADHD, then their capacity to focus and benefit from the program will be severely compromised (Hoggerman, Resnick, & Schnoll, 1993).

Programs, often associated with medical schools, are being developed around the country with an emphasis on the dual diagnosis of substance abuse and ADHD. This could be an excellent practice venue for psychologists who already have the training and experience in substance abuse treatment. In working with this dual-diagnosis population, there has been a general reluctance to provide such individuals with stimulant medication for fear of creating another addiction. This has not turned out to be the case. Most adults with ADHD and substance abuse histories have responded well to being prescribed stimulant medications as part of their overall treatment plans. Stimulant medications are important in the overall treatment of individuals with dual diagnosis, and concerns about abuse potential can be ameliorated by close monitoring and having a spouse or significant other attend follow-up sessions. The extent of this purported problem has been greatly overstated, to the detriment of some individuals' care. In fact, stimulant medication can lead to positive outcomes as part of an overall treatment plan.

LEARNING DISABILITY

Individuals with ADHD also commonly have LDs. LD encompasses a wide variety of disorders that affect an individual's ability to acquire and use listening, speaking, reading, writing, reasoning, or math skills (National Adult Literacy and Learning Disabilities Center, 1995). These problems vary in severity; may persist through adulthood; and may affect various areas of an individual's life, including learning, work, and social and emotional functioning. In children with ADHD, LDs have a greater-than-chance association, particularly reading disorder, disorder of written expression, and mathematics disorder. In adults with ADHD, the clinical manifestation of dyslexia frequently occurs (Wender, 1995, pp. 33, 35).

The cause of LD is unknown, and there are too many possibilities to consider before a cause can be pinned down with certainty. New evidence appears to show that most LDs are not caused by a single neurological problem in a specific area of the brain, but instead are caused from difficulties in bringing together information from various regions of the brain. Some researchers believe that LDs stem from subtle disturbances in brain structures and functions and that in many cases the disturbance begins before birth. Other factors that may influence the development of LD are genetic predisposition; tobacco, alcohol, and substance abuse by the mother prior to, during, and after pregnancy; problems during pregnancy or birth; and the emotional and physical environment (Jefferson Health System, 1997).

The amount of overlap between ADHD and LD is estimated from 10% to 90%, depending on the definition used. That is, some definitions are narrow and require specific statistical deficits in achievement with at least average intelligence, whereas others are broad, incorporating cultural variables, social class, and opportunity into the concept of LD. Still other definitions relate LD to emotional or conduct problems. Some literature has suggested that in an adult population with ADHD, almost half had needed tutoring during their elementary school years, and about a third had repeated a grade. For a subset of adults with LD, repeating the grade was due to conduct and behavior problems rather than to low academic achievement.

At least one national organization for people with LD has adopted as its definition of LD the ADHD criteria: If a person is impulsive, hyperactive, or inattentive, he or she by definition has LD. This is not accurate. Some individuals have ADHD and not LD, and some individuals have LD and not ADHD. There are still other individuals who have both ADHD and LD. It is important to be aware of LD in adults with ADHD because learning is an incremental and lifelong process, and LD may affect their daily lives long after they have completed their formal education.

Adults with LD face challenges in practically all aspects of life—in their family, education, employment, daily routines, and interpersonal relations. LD symptoms in adults could present as average or above-average ability but unexpected underachievement; problems with vision or hearing that are not the result of physical impairments; and behavioral or psychological manifestations—attention, concentration, and organization—that interfere with learning. In addition, error patterns in reading, writing, speaking, and math may help differentiate between possible LD and other causes of low achievement (Kerka, 1998). In regard to auditory processing, there are some individuals whose hearing apparatus is completely normal but who do not process auditory input properly. Thus, they can become confused and inattentive. If, during an evaluation, concerns surface about the person's ability to understand and process spoken information, and this is not based on any cognitive deficiency, then further consultation may be necessary to explore this problem.

Inattentive and distractible adults will often have problems in learning—on the job, in school, and at home. There are, however, a number of adults with ADHD who have problems of learning, or more accurately, with retaining what they have learned. Because individuals with ADHD have difficulties with attention, concentration, distractibility, and activity level, they will likely have problems retaining what they learn. Consider the child who is unable to spell words that were spelled perfectly the night before or the adult who cannot recall the order of presentation of a new product line.

NEUROBIOLOGY AND WOMEN

Neurobiobehavioral differences in gender significantly affect the clinician's ability to diagnose ADHD in women. For many the most damaging ADHD problems begin with puberty when women's monthly hormonal fluctuations commence. These fluctuations exacerbate the ADHD problems that they experience each month, particularly the week of their premenstrual phase, and continue to significantly affect them in adulthood. During this premenstrual phase, women with ADHD may experience significant to debilitating mood swings, anxiety, and depression. They report turbulent adolescent years. As their coping mechanisms become strained by the demands of schoolwork, new social interactions and expectations, decreasing family support, and increasing independence, underlying ADHD symptoms are exacerbated. Women with ADHD of the inattentive type have described their adolescent years as one of isolation and withdrawal. Others have reported going through phases of promiscuity and drug abuse. Thus, the complex interplay between the endocrinological and neurobiobehavioral environments may negatively affect a woman's inhibitory mechanisms already compromised by ADHD (Solden, 1995; Hallowell & Ratey, 1995, as cited in Solden, 1995).

The relationships between premenstrual syndrome (PMS) and ADHD and between menopause and ADHD are, at present, poorly understood and require more research. The fact remains, however, that for some women with ADHD, PMS or menopause tends to worsen their ADHD symptoms. For menopausal women, hormone replacement therapy appears to be effective in ameliorating restlessness, moodiness, and irritability, whether they stem from menopausal or ADHD symptoms.

OTHER BEHAVIORAL DISORDERS

This chapter has not included an exhaustive list of comorbid conditions and differential diagnoses because ADHD and other behavioral disorders are not mutually exclusive. Retardation and Tourette's syndrome also have been found to be comorbid conditions with ADHD (Blum, Cull, Braverman, & Comings, 1996; Comings et al., 1991). In addition, the clinician should be aware that any history of head trauma may produce problems with inattention, distractibility, impulsivity, lack of organization, hyperactivity, and other symptoms associated with ADHD (Niemann, Ruff, & Kramer, 1996; Gerring et al., 1998; Herskovits et al., 1999). Some recent evidence exists that people who have ADHD resulting from a head trauma may respond to treatments found effective for other individuals with ADHD (Mahalick et al., 1998). Seizure activity also requires thorough investigation. Individuals who experience brief, uncontrolled, and undiagnosed seizure activity such as petite mal or absence seizures may appear inattentive and distractible (Semrud-Clikeman & Wical, 1999). Finally, thyroid malfunction and early-onset Alzheimer's disease also can mimic ADHD (Barkley, 1998, p. 173).

Case Vignette: Edith

Edith, age 28, sought consultation because she had seen a television news show about adult ADHD, and the segment convinced her that she had it. She reported a history of underachievement and of failing 2nd and 4th grades. She graduated from high school in a more technical rather than academic program. She reported that there were many times when she just did not know where the class was with the lesson, had the wrong book or materials, or failed to hear the instructions. Diagnostic questionnaires, computerized assessment, and the history clearly suggested attention deficits.

However, during a 2-hour evaluation, there was recurrent evidence of a brief eye flutter, which would suggest an absence seizure. The therapist suggested to her that, although ADHD was a possibility, he was concerned about seizure activity. She was referred to a neurologist, who confirmed this and prescribed appropriate anticonvulsive medication. She is now working and attending junior college part-time.

Conclusion

ADHD in adulthood is a continuation of such symptoms from childhood; consequently, ADHD is similar in both groups. At present, the primary characteristics of ADHD and the diagnostic criteria officially used appear in the *DSM-IV*. However, although the *DSM-IV* diagnostic criteria were devised for both children and adults, the criteria have not been entirely useful in the diagnosis of adult ADHD. Problematic issues such as the need for more field trials for adult ADHD, the question of the cutoff point for diagnosis for children and adults, norms for clinical evaluation, the appropriateness of behavioral items used in the diagnostic criteria for different developmental periods, and symptoms in adults with ADHD not listed in *DSM-IV* have prompted the development of other diagnostic criteria for ADHD in adults, such as that developed by Hallowell and Ratey (1994) and Wender (1995). Thus, although the *DSM-IV* criteria represent the most specific, reliable, empirically based criteria for ADHD currently available, practitioners should exercise their clinical judgment in adopting it and making necessary adjustments in applying it, particularly in evaluating adult ADHD.

In addition, differential diagnosis and evaluation of comorbidity can be the most difficult aspects of diagnosis, assessment, and treatment of ADHD in adults. Clinicians need to have familiarity and experience with the broad spectrum of mental disorders that present with ADHD (i.e., comorbidity) and to be able to differentiate other conditions that mimic "true" ADHD (i.e., differential diagnosis). It is worth repeating that all ADHD symptoms can be observed in a non-ADHD population. It is the severity, intensity, and the degree of interference in the individual's life that moves the inattentiveness, forgetfulness, and hyperactivity associated with today's lifestyle to that of an ADHD diagnosis.

References and Resources

American Psychiatric Association. (1980). *Diagnostic and statistical manual of mental disorders* (3rd ed.). Washington, DC: Author.

American Psychiatric Association. (1987). *Diagnostic and statistical manual of mental disorders* (3rd ed., rev.). Washington, DC: Author.

American Psychiatric Association. (1994). *Diagnostic and statistical manual of mental disorders* (4th ed.). Washington, DC: Author.

Barkley, R. A. (1998). *Attention-deficit-hyperactivity disorder: A handbook for diagnosis and treatment* (2nd ed.). New York: Guilford Press.

Biederman, J., Faraone, S., Mick, E., Moore, P., & Lelon, E. (1996). Child Behavior Checklist findings further support comorbidity between ADHD and major depression in a referred sample. *Journal of the American Academy of Child and Adolescent Psychiatry, 35,* 734–742.

Biederman, J., Newcorn, J., & Sprich, S. (1991). Comorbidity of attention deficit hyperactivity disorder with conduct, depressive, anxiety, and other disorders. *American Journal of Psychiatry, 148,* 564–577.

Blum, K., Cull, J. G., Braverman, E. R., & Comings, D. E. (1996). Reward deficiency syndrome. *American Scientist, 84*(2), 132–145.

Bohline, D. S. (1985). Intellectual and effective characteristics of attention deficit disordered children. *Journal of Learning Disabilities, 18,* 604–608.

Breen, M. J., & Barkley, R. A. (1983). The Personality Inventory for Children (PIC): Its clinical utility with hyperactive children. *Journal of Pediatric Psychology, 8,* 359–366.

Breen, M., & Barkley, R. (1984). Psychological adjustment in learning disabled, hyperactive, and hyperactive/learning disabled children using the Personality Inventory for Children. *Journal of Clinical Child Psychology, 13,* 232–236.

Cantwell, D. P. (1996). Attention deficit disorder: A review of the past 10 years. *Journal of the American Academy of Child and Adolescent Psychiatry, 35,* 978–987.

Comings et al. (1991). The dopamine D2 receptor locus as a modifying gene in neuropsychiatric disorders. *Journal of the American Medical Association, 266,* 1793–1800.

Cook, J. (1997). *The book of positive quotations.* Minneapolis, MN: Fairview Press.

Gerring, J. P., Brady, K. P., Chen, A., Vasa, R., Grados, M., Bandeen-Roche, K. J., Bryan, R. N., & Denckla, M. B. (1998). Premorbid prevalence of ADHD and development of secondary ADHD after closed head injury. *Journal of the American Academy of Child and Adolescent Psychiatry, 37*(6), 647–654.

Hallowell, E. M., & Ratey, J. J. (1995). *Answers to distraction.* New York: Pantheon Books.

Herskovits, E. H., Megalooikonomou, V., Davatzikos, C., Chen, A., Bryan, R. N., & Gerring, J. P. (1999). Is the spatial distribution of brain lesions associated with closed-head injury predictive of subsequent development of attention-deficit/hyperactivity disorder? Analysis with brain-image database. *Radiology, 213*(2), 389–394.

Hoggerman, G. S., Resnick, R. J., & Schnoll, S. H. (1993). Attention deficits in newly abstinent substance abusers: Childhood recollections and attention performance in 39 subjects. *Journal of Addictive Diseases, 12,* 37–53.

Jefferson Health System. (1997). *Learning disabilities—Cause. Mental health disorders at Jefferson Health System.* Available online at www.jeffersonhealth.org/diseases/mental_health/ldcause.htm

Jensen, J. B., Burke, N., & Garfinkel, B. D. (1988). Depression and symptoms of attention deficit disorder with hyperactivity. *Journal of the American Academy of Child and Adolescent Psychiatry, 27,* 742–747.

Jensen, P. S., Martin, D., & Cantwell, D. P. (1997). Comorbidity in ADHD: Implications for research, practice, and DSM-V. *Journal of the American Academy of Child and Adolescent Psychiatry, 36,* 1065–1079.

Kerka, S. (1998). *Adults with learning disabilities* (ERIC Digest No. 189). ERIC Clearinghouse on Adult, Career, and Vocational Education, Columbus, OH. Available online at www.ldonline.org/ld_indepth/adult/eric189.html

Mahalick, D. M., Carmel, P. W., Greenberg, J. P., Molofsky, W., Brown, J. A., Heary, R. F., Marks, D., Zampella, E., Hodosh, R., & von der Schmidt, E., III. (1998). Psychopharmacologic treatment of acquired attention disorders in children with brain injury. *Pediatric Neurosurgery, 29*(3), 121–126.

National Adult Literacy and Learning Disabilities Center. (1995). *Adults with learning disabilities: Definitions and issues* (ED 387 989). Washington, DC: Author.

Niemann, H., Ruff, R. M., & Kramer, J. H. (1996). An attempt towards differentiating attentional deficits in traumatic brain injury. *Neuropsychology Review, 6*(1), 11–46.

Semrud-Clikeman, M., & Wical, B. (1999). Components of attention in children with complex partial seizures with and without ADHD. *Epilepsia, 40*(2), 211–215.

Solden, S. (1995). *Women with attention deficit disorder.* Grass Valley, CA: Underwood Books.

Szatmari, P., Offord, D. R., & Boyle, M. H. (1989). Ontario child health study: Prevalence of attention deficit disorder with hyperactivity. *Journal of Child Psychology and Psychiatry, 30,* 219–230.

Tzelepis, A., Schubinger, H., & Warbasse, L. H. (1995). Differential diagnosis and psychiatric comorbidity patterns in adult attention deficit disorder. In K. Nadeau (Ed.), *A comprehensive guide to attention deficit disorder in adults* (pp. 35–48). New York: Brunner/Mazel.

Weiss, M., Hechtman, L. T., & Weiss, G. (1999). *ADHD in adulthood: A guide to current theory, diagnosis, and treatment.* Baltimore: Johns Hopkins University Press.

Wender, P. H. (1995). *Attention-deficit-hyperactivity disorders in adulthood.* New York: Oxford University Press.

World Health Organization. (1992). *International classification of diseases* (10th ed.). Geneva, Switzerland: Author.

Assessment | 5

On the human chess board, all moves are possible.
　　　　　　　　　　　　　　　　—Miriam Schiff

This chapter discusses techniques for assessing the existence of core ADHD symptoms in adults. Assessment consists of two parts: (a) the process of obtaining a reliable and valid retrospective and current history of the patient that will lead to a credible evaluation and (b) the methods or tools that will enhance the reliability and validity of the diagnostic conclusions, such as psychological and educational testing, rating scales, and computerized-assessment techniques. Above all, assessment should be guided by four core considerations of adult ADHD.

Core Considerations in Diagnosing Adult ADHD

Barkley (1998) provided a general strategy for diagnosing ADHD by outlining "tighter" conceptual criteria for the disorder. The assessment process should aim to generate enough data and evidence to reliably answer four core questions:

1. Is there credible evidence that the patient experienced ADHD-type symptoms in early childhood that, at least by the middle school years, led to substantial and chronic impairment across settings?
2. Is there credible evidence that ADHD-type symptoms currently cause the patient substantial and consistent impairment across settings?

3. Are there explanations other than ADHD that better account for the clinical picture?
4. For patients who meet criteria for ADHD, is there evidence for the existence of comorbid conditions? (p. 349).

All procedures used for obtaining patient information during the diagnostic process should be aimed at reliably answering these four fundamental questions. However, it is important to keep in mind that it is not always possible, due to poor memory, poor record keeping, or other circumstances, to find ADHD symptoms in childhood.

Translating process and method into an actual clinical situation, Weiss, Hechtman, and Weiss (1999) provided a useful outline for assessment:

1. interviewing
2. reviewing symptoms of ADHD and using rating scales and computerized-assessment techniques
3. assessing for comorbid psychiatric diagnoses
4. taking a thorough history, beginning in childhood
5. referring for consultation, if necessary
6. assessing impairment.

These steps need not be followed in sequence. The practitioner adapts them according to whatever is efficient, comfortable, and works best for practitioner and patient.

The Intake Process

INTAKE QUESTIONS

Most practitioners at the time of registering a patient ask questions regarding the problems that prompted him or her to seek professional care. Most often these intake questions include a checklist with general questions about problems related to work, school, sleep, appetite, and so forth. This format is ideal for adding questions regarding inattention, concentration, distractibility, lack of focus, messiness, forgetfulness, and procrastination. It may even be helpful for practitioners to operationalize some of the *DSM-IV* criteria in their own wording and use them as screening questions. During the clinical interviews, the practitioner can review the intake form, note the checked-off problem areas, and use this as a basis for probing situations in which ADHD-like symptoms may pose problems for the patient, considering a range of areas across daily life.

OBSERVATIONS

As part of the initial intake, the clinician attends to any random motions and motor discharge that the patient may make, recalling that hyper-activity is better conceived as movement when there does not need to be any, rather than as an ongoing motor activity. Fidgety as well as talkative people can be hyperactive. Many adults who have attention deficits will report their difficulty in remaining seated and completing tasks.

During the course of the initial diagnostic interview, it is important to make note of eye contact and observe whether the patient is avoiding or unable to maintain eye contact. Many individuals with ADHD will have difficulty making eye contact, not because of suspiciousness, shame, or guilt, but because they are distracted by other things in the practitioner's office. I describe these individuals as having "radar-eyes" because they seem to scan the office, from wall plaques to photographs to items on the desk to books on the bookcase and so on, and rarely cast their eyes downward. Because individuals with ADHD frequently have difficulty screening out irrelevant and unnecessary stimuli, they may be continually drawn to stimuli in the practitioner's office.

PROBING FOR COMMON PROBLEMS

Asking how a spouse, friend, or employer might describe the person can be very instructive, especially for issues of attention, distractibility, im-pulsivity, and activity level. Many important areas of the patient's functioning, such as interpersonal relationships, sexual functioning, parenting, work and employment history, financial management, and day-to-day activities, can best be assessed by interviewing the patient's significant others.

It is important to obtain descriptions of how the patient's desk, bed-room or bathroom, and other personal space looks in terms of neatness or messiness. There is some evidence to suggest that the most common problem, although it is not always described as such, is difficulty with organization. Patients and often others complain about messiness and not being able to find things. Piles of "stuff" are in closets, under beds, and in drawers; sometimes, individuals with ADHD simply move these piles from one place to another, making no progress in reducing the quantity or organizing it.

Likewise, it is important to ask about the patient's daily schedule and whether or not he or she gets done during the day what he or she planned to do. The list of things that do not get done usually includes those that could significantly benefit the person to complete, such as meeting sales quotas to qualify for bonuses, submitting project reports on time, doing activities that could significantly improve marital or interpersonal relationships, and even finishing tasks that relate to personal hobbies. Individuals with ADHD are well intentioned but, by and large, may not be able meet deadlines, fulfill commitments and promises, or complete tasks with any degree of consistency. They are, at other times, described as "forgetful." They may present these problems not because they feel guilty or ashamed, but rather because they are dumbfounded by their behavior and do not understand why they do what they do. Such behavior initially may be interpreted as self-defeating, but when it carries over to pleasurable and desirable activities, and when the individual registers perplexity more than affect, such behavior could be another manifestation of ADHD disorganization.

For example, Steven, age 28, calls his father (this author) who lives in another state to tell him that the company that Steven works for is relocating from Georgia to Florida. Steven is very excited about the move and has much to tell me. However, he needs to call back to do so and promises to call later that afternoon. I state that I'll be in all afternoon and will await his call. However, I am not surprised when he does not call until five days later still full of enthusiasm for the move. I remind Steven that he promised to call earlier; he apologizes and states that he was just "being myself." Steven knows that he has difficulty accessing working memory and no longer gets defensive about these errors in time and organization; he calls himself "Mr. Forgetful."

Thus, it is useful to explore the pattern of work effort (and outcome) over the course of the day. A low energy level can be seen as problematic for many adults with ADHD, which can cause difficulties both at home and the office. The patient may become tired during the day, as difficulties meeting deadlines and other commitments increase. A related behavior that may be observed in some patients is a great difficulty in getting started on a task despite repeated prodding and reminding. Both of these patterns look like procrastination, but in individuals with ADHD the cause of such behavior lies within the ADHD symptom cluster.

Inattentive adults, more so than either hyperactive or combined type, show an irritability and affective lability often accompanied by sensitivity to criticism. Questions need to be asked to determine the history and severity of these symptoms and their context. Difficulty explaining these behaviors and being bewildered by them are characteristic reactions of individuals with ADHD.

Women with ADHD are often encumbered by their disorganized behavior in terms of their traditional role as homemakers. Despite changing attitudes toward work, household chores, and family roles of men and women, in many American families the major household tasks and child-rearing activities still fall to the woman, whether or not she works outside the home. Whereas men with ADHD may have superorganized wives who can efficiently manage day-to-day affairs of work, family, and home, women with ADHD are less likely to have husbands who can and will organize home and family. Clinicians should be sensitive to comments from their female patients (or from their spouses) about late dinners, a disorganized household, an inability to entertain at home, and issues around child rearing; all should be evaluated as possible evidence of ADHD. Many women with ADHD, feeling that they cannot meet societal expectations, often experience problems with depression and self-esteem.

RELATED QUESTIONS

In the course of these initial contacts, the clinician will want to evaluate, in addition to the four core symptoms of ADHD, the patient's use of leisure time, stress tolerance, and anger management. Individuals with ADHD often have difficulty doing things productively in their leisure time. More important, they do not handle stress well, even routine stresses. They can be very sensitive to criticism and perceived pressure from others. Because individuals with ADHD tend to be very reactive, they are quick to anger (and also quick to calm down). Thus, a common difficult marital situation can be one in which a spouse with ADHD has completely forgotten a disagreement, while the spouse without ADHD is still fuming.

RETROSPECTIVE HISTORY

How the adult patient was perceived in childhood by teachers and parents during the elementary and middle school years (and beyond) is an important component of the intake history. In the early part of the assessment, it is helpful to obtain a detailed educational history from the patient. One should review both school-based behaviors as well as performance. Information from the patient's former elementary school teachers could be very instructive; the patient should bring in whatever report cards, teacher commentaries, and such that the family has saved. If information is still unclear, one should consider the possibility of arranging a session with the patient's parents. If direct contact with parents is inappropriate or not possible, the clinician can request the patient to ask his or her parents about his or her behavior as a school-age child or even seek such information from an older sibling if the parents are no longer living.

Many children with ADHD may do well in the early grades but begin to experience academic problems in the 3rd or 4th grade. This is because teaching methods in most school systems undergo changes in the middle of elementary school. By the 4th grade, there is less repetition and drill and more emphasis on independent learning and organizational skills. Thus, at this point, the negative impact of ADHD is manifested in the school performance and secondarily in behavioral reactions to the increased academic demands and greater stress.

Middle school also may be another important marker in the patient's educational experience. In elementary school, the child was used to more stability, with one or two classrooms and teachers (often with the teacher, not the students, changing classrooms). In middle school, the child most typically moves among five to seven classrooms and teachers. The process of changing classes places greater demands on the child's attention and organizational skills. The changing classroom, classmates, and teachers (along with a demand of physically moving to a new location) also increase the stress experienced by the child. Similarly, the change from middle school to high school can strain some teenager's attention for the first time, causing academic and personal problems as academic pressures increase and supports decrease.

Clinicians should note whether the patient exhibited behavioral and academic problems in elementary school but seemed to improve in high school. There can be, with maturation, some reduction in the severity and frequency of ADHD symptoms. Such adults also may report "turning around" in high school, because, with neurobiological maturation, the symptom cluster of hyperactivity–impulsivity may lessen for some individuals. With a reduction in the expression of these symptoms, improved academic performance can follow, and behavioral improvement in the form of fewer conduct problems may result as well.

Case Vignette: Harold

At the time of intake, Harold, age 44, was retired from the navy, married, and had 2 children. He was becoming increasingly depressed about his inability to adapt to civilian life. He had had an excellent naval career but an unusual beginning. Harold had quit high school because he was "a poor, dumb student." His teachers often described him as "mentally lazy," with much more academic promise than he showed in his grades. He was uninterested and unmotivated in school, but he did not have behavior or conduct problems. He enlisted in the navy shortly after his 18th birthday, somewhere between the 9th and 10th grade.

After his first 4-year enlistment, he was tested for the nuclear navy, and he re-enlisted for an additional 6 years to obtain specialized training. When asked whether he noted any difference between his initial and re-enlistment years, he said that he noticed for the first time that he read and remembered more information from newspaper articles. Before the re-enlistment, at the encouragement of his wife, he took the high school equivalency exam and passed it on his first attempt. He said no one was more surprised than he, although, he added with a smile, his wife was not. His passing the exam enabled him to not only get into the nuclear navy, but also to stay with that area of specialization. Harold began to find reading "fun," began taking college courses over the next 12 years, and completed a bachelor's degree.

After 25 years in the navy, Harold, encouraged by his wife, decided to retire so that he could spend more time with her and their teenage children. Because of his training, he was recruited by a nuclear power company before his discharge. At first, Harold's difficulties at work were thought to be just a matter of fitting into the new system. However, as the months went by, it was clear that he was having major problems with his new duties as well as with the additional commitments to his wife and sons. He was stressed because of what he saw as the lack of clarity in his new job and its organizational structure. He was tense and frustrated at home and short-tempered with his sons. He had ongoing difficulty with details both at home and at work, which he thought was just his "forgetfulness."

Harold's history suggests ADHD. Harold did not want to take medication; instead, a combination of marital therapy, bibliotherapy for both him and his wife, and behavioral interventions to protect some of his time at work were successful. Treatment focused on Harold's problem with sustained attention. His office was redesigned with fewer distractions. His fish tank was removed (he liked it because it reminded him of the navy), as he would frequently find himself looking at it rather than at his work. His desk was arranged so that his back was to the window. Specific times were set aside for Harold to review the work of his subordinates, and he blocked out specific times for attending to subordinates' questions and problems and returning nonurgent telephone calls. Last, when he was at work, his secretary screened his pages. This arrangement caused some problems and concerns early on, but within 4 weeks the behavioral interventions were working smoothly.

MEDICAL AND WORK RECORDS

As part of a comprehensive assessment, it is useful to review with the patient both medical and work histories. As with the educational review, this review can be more productive if it is based in part on copies of medical reports and work performance evaluations. The patient's recall and experience are important, but reviewing the actual documents may reveal details or events that the patient may have forgotten or was embarrassed to mention.

The patient being evaluated for ADHD should not have any biological impairment that might cause ADHD-like symptoms. If the patient has had a head trauma or a history of seizures, then a referral to other specialists such as a neuropsychologist or a neurologist is essential to help clarify diagnosis and treatment. In most cases, neuropsychological assessment has not been helpful in confirming or negating an ADHD diagnosis, but it may be helpful when neurological deficits are suspected. This is equally true for electroencephalograms. In general, these procedures are usually unnecessary unless results of the intake evaluation raise questions that need to be answered by these procedures.

A number of adults with ADHD also have difficulty with sleep. This may take the form of early-morning awakening as well as difficulty falling asleep. The latter is often the result of the patient being unable to temporarily forget events of the day or to stop anticipating the next day's events. It may be necessary to refer the patient to a sleep disorder program as part of the management of ADHD.

DRUG HISTORY

The taking of a drug history should be a standard part of any initial evaluation. Often drug experimentation is a significant finding among teenagers and adults with undiagnosed ADHD. Individuals with ADHD tend to experiment with certain drugs and to avoid others. Of importance in assessing ADHD is the patient's response to amphetamines or other psychostimulants. An individual who tries, and subsequently stays away from, stimulants because he or she did not experience a "buzz" or "rush" may possibly have ADHD. However, if a person does "get high" on speed, it does not eliminate ADHD as a diagnosis. Depending on dosage strength, virtually everyone has some improved concentration when taking a stimulant. However, among a drug-abusing population, individuals who avoid stimulants because of a "paradoxical response" may have ADHD.

Case Vignette: Ariel

Ariel, age 18, was admitted to an inpatient dual diagnosis program at a large metropolitan medical center. It was difficult to find a substance that Ariel had not tried and enjoyed. She would use virtually any drug that anyone offered her. After enumerating her drug experience and before the clinician could probe further, she said to the interviewer "I don't do speed!" Asked why not by the clinician, Ariel responded that she had tried speed once and while everyone else was "up and roaring," she sat down and read a magazine. She said that she could not wait for that "lousy drug" to wear off.

Protocols

The clinical interview is essential to a comprehensive evaluation and diagnosis (Weiss et al., 1999). In addition, although there is no definitive test for diagnosing ADHD, clinicians can use various scales and protocols to enhance the assessment process. Most of these are psychological, neuropsychological, and educational tests and computerized tests of attention.

INTERVIEW PROTOCOLS AND RATING SCALES

Several published guides and semistructured interviews for history-taking for adults with ADHD are available to assist the clinician in the collection of relevant data. For example, some clinicians find the Barkley (1998) guide user-friendly, detailed, specific, and comprehensive for purposes of data collection. The guide provides a self-report form that the patient can complete covering his or her developmental, employment, health, and social history. It also includes an adult interview aimed at generating information on the patient's family history, school history, and family psychiatric history. Because it is detailed and comprehensive, the practitioner is less likely to omit or miss relevant detailed information.

The Conners (1994) Adult ADHD History Form is another history-taking booklet that can be completed by the patient prior to the evaluation or used by the clinician as a guide to data collecting. There is also the ADD Diagnostic Form by Brown (1996) that has separate versions for adults and adolescents. The Conners and Brown protocols are not as specific, detailed, or comprehensive as Barkley's guide, but both are often sufficient for routine general practice.

Other ADHD scales and guides include the Semi-structured Interview for Adult ADHD (Nadeau, 1991), the Attention-Deficit Scales for Adults (Triolo & Murphy, 1996), and the Wender (1995) Utah Rating Scale that discriminates ADHD from depression (see chapter 4 for Wender's Utah Criteria for ADHD). Most of these scales are available from the ADD WareHouse catalog (see the Appendix).

These scales and other protocols may help the practitioner focus on a review of symptoms that would be part of an overall assessment addressing the question of attention deficits. Most of these scales have operationalized *DSM-IV* criteria or other behaviors seen in an ADHD population. The rating scales have normative-based cutoff scores; once the scales are completed and scored, they are compared to the scores of individuals who have been diagnosed as having ADHD. When possible, it is beneficial to have the patient's spouse, parent, supervisor, or others who know the patient well also complete a rating scale on the patient, as it provides valuable information about how other people see the patient (and around which behaviors the perceptions of the patient as compared to others are similar or dissimilar). These behavioral rating scales can be administered as frequently as necessary for monitoring the therapeutic process, as well as for monitoring medication and treatment effectiveness.

COMPUTERIZED TESTS OF ATTENTION

Several computerized tests are helpful in identifying adults with ADHD, and these are commercially available. Some include the Test of Variables of Attention (Greenberg & Dupuy, 1988–1993), the Gordon Diagnostic System (1983), the Integrated Visual and Auditory Continuous Performance Test (IVA; Sanford & Turner, 1996), and the Conners Continuous Performance Test (CPT, 1995).

All of these instruments address issues of inattention, impulsivity, and distractibility, along with the capacity to maintain attention over time. These tests also have been shown to be responsive to medication management with adults with ADHD. That is, performance often improves on these measures in a linear relationship to medication dosage. However, these procedures have difficulty distinguishing between depression-based and ADHD-based concentration problems. None address the other symptoms of ADHD.

It should be emphasized that these electronic tests are not diagnostic instruments per se, but when appropriately used, they can provide additional information that is useful in the diagnostic and outcome assessment processes (Greenhill et al., 1996). Their predictive power varies according to a variety of factors, including the nature of the comparison groups (Weiss et al., 1999). Thus, a test can discriminate better between an individual with ADHD and one without ADHD than between an individual with ADHD and another with many other clinical syndromes. For example, the CPT is believed to be most discriminating for individuals between ages 6 and 17; within this age group, the CPT index is reported to have identified between 70% and 85% of individuals with ADHD relative to the general population (Weiss et al., 1999).

I have had good results using the CPT, but I have not used the other tests. There are false-negative results with the CPT, but very few false-positive results. The CPT can be acquired for a single purchase price, and the clinician has unlimited use of the procedure.

PSYCHOLOGICAL TESTING

Intellectual testing may be helpful, at least on a screening level, to determine general intelligence, but full IQ assessment generally provides minimal discriminative information in making the diagnosis of ADHD. In certain instances, it may be necessary to complete both intelligence and achievement tests to rule out potential LD when this cannot be deduced from the educational history. In addition, there are times when it is necessary for treatment planning to evaluate academic achievement in light of intellectual potential.

Depending on the evaluation and clarity of the diagnoses, there may be a need to complete further psychological assessment. The MMPI–2 (Hathaway & McKinley, 1989), Millon tests (Millon, 1993, 1994; Millon, Green, & Meagher, 1977, 1982), or similar instruments may be helpful, when necessary, to clarify a comorbid condition or a condition that presents with problems of attention. Projective assessment is less often beneficial.

Assessment of Comorbid Conditions

Comorbidity of other mental health disorders with ADHD can be as high as 77% (Biederman et al., 1993). In assessing an adult for ADHD, it is important to rule out other behavioral disorders, including those that usually present in childhood (such as LD, Tourette's syndrome, oppositional disorder, conduct disorder, and Asperger syndrome), as well as those that generally present in adulthood (such as affective disorders, anxiety disorders, substance abuse, and personality disorders; see Weiss et al., 1999).

Determining common comorbid conditions of ADHD in adults is not too difficult because these conditions are generally familiar to both patients and clinicians. A rigorous mental status examination is frequently sufficient. In addition, many standardized instruments are available for this purpose. These include the Symptom Checklist–90-R (Derogatis, 1975), the Beck Depression Inventory–II (Beck & Steer, 1996), the Hamilton Rating Scale for Depression (Hamilton, 1960), and the Hamilton Rating Scale for Anxiety (Hamilton, 1959; see also Weiss et al., 1999).

Rather, the difficult task for the clinician is assessing comorbid conditions that first present in childhood. Such conditions often resurface in adulthood as residual impairment from the childhood diagnosis. No reliable adult norms currently exist to diagnose or rate the residual impairment, and it is difficult to obtain a sufficiently detailed self-report from the patient or sufficiently detailed information from parents or teachers regarding symptoms that occurred during the patient's early developmental years. Currently, we do not have standardized rating scales for assessing adults for conduct disorder, oppositional disorder, or Tourette's syndrome. Furthermore, assessing LD in adulthood is difficult. In addition, none of the semistructured interviews used in research and epidemiological studies screen out the residual impairment associated with childhood disorders. However, there is some empirical evidence that comorbid patterns that exist in adults with ADHD appear to be similar to those manifested in children with ADHD. Checkmate Plus is currently developing an adult symptom checklist for assessing ADHD and comorbid conditions for use by clinicians (see Weiss et al., 1999, pp. 61–62).

Conclusion

Assessing an adult for ADHD symptoms presents a formidable challenge for clinicians for various reasons. As Barkley (1998) pointed out, the fact that most people experience ADHD-like symptoms to some degree, the high degree of comorbidity, and the lack of a "litmus test" for ADHD are some of the major complexities that make assessment of ADHD difficult. However, this does not mean that adult ADHD defies diagnosis. A comprehensive and thoughtful assessment by a sufficiently trained and experienced clinician is required. Such an evaluation may take into account critical aspects of the patient's childhood and early adult history, current functioning, degree of impairment, comorbidity, and the presence of symptoms that may mimic ADHD.

In general, in evaluating adults for potential attention deficits, the clinician must be able to identify a childhood onset. Clinicians should then focus on the four core symptoms and determine to what extent they impair the adult's functioning at school, work, home, and leisure pursuits. The information gathered by the clinician should include diagnostic questionnaires and other procedures that will help clarify and discriminate among several possible diagnoses. Finally, it is important to evaluate possible comorbid conditions, as most adults with ADHD will have additional difficulties.

Mental health practitioners also should be reminded that when other evaluations need to be done (neuropsychological, neurological, medical, educational, or career), they as the primary clinicians should maintain case management responsibility for patient treatment. Professionals to whom the patient is referred must understand that they are consultants. As the primary treating clinician, the practitioner will accumulate whatever consultation may be necessary and appropriate and use the information in developing a multipronged treatment plan. If such a plan utilizes ongoing pharmacological management, collaboration with primary care physicians is necessary. In my experience, most pediatricians, family physicians, and internists who treat ADHD are more than willing to collaborate with mental health practitioners.

References and Resources

American Psychiatric Association. (1994). *Diagnostic and statistical manual of mental disorders* (4th ed.). Washington, DC: Author.

Barkley, R. A. (1998). *Attention-deficit-hyperactivity disorder: A handbook for diagnosis and treatment* (2nd ed.). New York: Guilford Press.

Beck, A. T., & Steer, R. A. (1996). *The Beck depression inventory–II.* San Antonio, TX: Psychological Corporation.

Biederman, J., Faraone, S. V., Spencer, T., Wilens, T., Norman, D., Lapey, K. A., Mick, E., Lehman, B. K., & Doyle, A. (1993). Patterns of psychiatric comorbidity, cognition, and psychosocial functioning in adults with attention deficit hyperactivity disorder. *American Journal of Psychiatry, 150,* 1792–1798.

Brown, T. E. (1996). *Brown Attention-Deficit Disorder Scales Manual.* San Antonio, TX: Psychological Corporation.

Conners, C. K. (1994). *Conners Adult ADHD History Form.* North Tonawanda, NY: Multi-Health Systems.

Conners, C. K. (1995). *The Conners Continuous Performance Test (CPT).* North Tonawanda, NY: Multi-Health Systems.

Cook, J. (1997). *The book of positive quotations.* Minneapolis, MN: Fairview Press.

Derogatis, L. R. (1975). *Symptom checklist–90-Revised.* Eden Prairie, MN: National Computer Systems, Inc.

Gordon, M. (1983). *The Gordon Diagnostic System.* DeWitt, NY: Gordon Systems.

Greenberg, L. M., & Dupuy, T. R. (1988–1993). *Test of Variables of Attention (TOVA).* Los Alamos, CA: Universal Attention Disorders.

Greenhill, L., Conners, C. K., Gordon, M., Cantwell, D., & Wells, K. (1996). *The measurement of attention in office practice: An aid to treatment.* Symposium 21: Proceedings of the 43rd Annual Meeting of the American Academy of Child and Adolescent Psychiatry, Philadelphia.

Hamilton, M. (1959). The assessment of anxiety states by rating. *British Journal of Medical Psychology, 32,* 50–55.

Hamilton, M. (1960). Rating scale for depression. *Journal of Neurology, Neurosurgery, and Psychiatry, 23,* 56–61.

Hathaway, S. R., & McKinley, J. C. (1989). *Minnesota multiphasic personality inventory–2.* Minneapolis: University of Minnesota Press.

Millon, T. (1993). *Millon adolescent clinical inventory*. Eden Prairie, MN: National Computer Systems, Inc.

Millon, T. (1994). *Millon clinical multiaxial inventory–III*. Eden Prairie, MN: National Computer Systems, Inc.

Millon, T., Green, C. J., & Meagher, R. B., Jr. (1977). *Millon adolescent personality inventory*. Eden Prairie, MN: National Computer Systems, Inc.

Millon, T., Green, C. J., & Meagher, R. B., Jr. (1982). *Millon behavioral health inventory*. Eden Prairie, MN: National Computer Systems, Inc.

Nadeau, K. G. (1991). *Adult ADHD Questionnaire*. Silver Spring, MD: Chesapeake Psychological Services of Maryland.

Sanford, J. A., & Turner, A. (1996). *Integrated visual and auditory continuous performance test*. Richmond, VA: Author.

Triolo, S. J., & Murphy, K. R. (1996). *Attention-deficit scales for adults*. Bristol, PA: Brunner/Mazel.

Weiss, M., Hechtman, L. T., & Weiss, G. (1999). *ADHD in adulthood: A guide to current theory, diagnosis, and treatment*. Baltimore: Johns Hopkins University Press.

Wender, P. H. (1995). *Attention-deficit-hyperactivity disorders in adulthood*. New York: Oxford University Press.

Diagnosis, Medical Management, Referral, and Reimbursement

6

Statistics are no substitute for judgment.
—Henry Clay

As noted from the previous chapters, adult ADHD is frequently a hidden disorder. In chapter 4, I provided an overview of diagnostic criteria currently used for adult ADHD, differential diagnoses, and comorbid disorders. I outlined the generally accepted *DSM-IV* diagnostic criteria and two other diagnostic criteria specifically developed for adult ADHD. In chapter 5, I provided an overview of the criteria domains of functioning and specific behaviors that needed consideration as part of an initial assessment of possible ADHD in adults. This chapter discusses how the practitioner applies ADHD criteria in actually making a diagnosis, the implications of the diagnosis for medication management referral, and the practical matters of reimbursement and billing.

The DSM-IV: *The Medically Accepted Diagnostic Criteria for ADHD*

It may be helpful, at least when clinicians begin evaluating for and in formulating a diagnosis of ADHD, to use the *DSM-IV* criteria as a guideline (see Exhibit 6.1). However, clinicians should remember an impor-

EXHIBIT 6.1

DSM-IV Criteria for ADHD

A. Either (1) or (2):
   (1) Six (or more) of the following symptoms of *inattention* have persisted for at
       least 6 months to a degree that is maladaptive and inconsistent with
       developmental level:
       Inattention
       (a) often fails to give close attention to details or makes careless mistakes in
           schoolwork, work, or other activities
       (b) often has difficulty sustaining attention in tasks or play activities
       (c) often does not seem to listen when spoken to directly
       (d) often does not follow through on instructions and fails to finish schoolwork,
           chores, or duties in the workplace (not due to oppositional behavior or
           failure to understand instructions)
       (e) often has difficulty organizing tasks and activities
       (f) often avoids, dislikes, or is reluctant to engage in tasks that require sustained
           mental effort (such as schoolwork or homework)
       (g) often loses things necessary for tasks or activities (e.g., toys, school
           assignments, pencils, books, or tools)
       (h) is often easily distracted by extraneous stimuli
       (i) is often forgetful in daily activities
   (2) Six (or more) of the following symptoms of *hyperactivity–impulsivity* have
       persisted for at least 6 months to a degree that is maladaptive and inconsistent
       with developmental level:
       Hyperactivity
       (a) often fidgets with hands or feet or squirms in seat
       (b) often leaves seat in classroom or in other situations in which remaining
           seated is expected
       (c) often runs about or climbs excessively in situations in which it is
           inappropriate (in adolescents or adults, may be limited to subjective feelings
           of restlessness)
       (d) often has difficulty playing or engaging in leisure activities quietly
       (e) is often "on the go" or often acts as if "driven by a motor"
       (f) often talks excessively
       Impulsivity
       (g) often blurts out answers before the questions have been completed
       (h) often has difficulty awaiting turn
       (i) often interrupts or intrudes on others (e.g., butts into conversations or
           games)
B. Some hyperactive–impulsive or inattentive symptoms that caused impairment were
   present before age 7 years.
C. Some impairment from the symptoms is present in two or more settings (e.g., at
   school [or work] and at home).
D. There must be clear evidence of clinically significant impairment in social, academic,
   or occupational functioning.
E. The symptoms do not occur exclusively during the course of a Pervasive
   Developmental Disorder, Schizophrenia, or other Psychotic Disorder and are not
   better accounted for by another mental disorder (e.g., Mood Disorder, Anxiety
   Disorder, Dissociative Disorder, or a Personality Disorder).

(continued)

E X H I B I T   6 . 1   **continued**

Code based on type:
314.01   Attention-Deficit/Hyperactivity Disorder, Combined Type: if both Criteria A1 and A2 are met for the past 6 months.
314.00   Attention-Deficit/Hyperactivity Disorder, Predominantly Inattentive Type: if Criterion A1 is met, but Criterion A2 is not met for the past 6 months.
314.01   Attention-Deficit/Hyperactivity Disorder, Predominantly Hyperactive–Impulsive Type: if Criterion A2 is met, but Criterion A1 is not met for the past 6 months.
Coding note: For individuals (especially adolescents and adults) who currently have symptoms that no longer meet full criteria, "In Partial Remission" should be specified.

Note. From *Diagnostic and Statistical Manual of Mental Disorders* (4th ed., pp. 83–85), by the American Psychiatric Association, 1994, Washington, DC: Author. Copyright 1994 by the American Psychiatric Association. Reprinted with permission.

tant point: The *DSM-IV* criteria were developed by a subcommittee of the group examining disorders that are usually found in childhood. This subgroup was charged to look at "disruptive disorders," one of which was ADHD. The resultant criteria are the consequences of the discussions and compromises of that working group on disruptive disorders after their review of the literature. Thus, the clinician should not be bound by them.

The *DSM-IV* criteria are no more absolute than is 98.6°F always the "normal" temperature of a human being, with 98.7° always being a fever to be treated or, even more absurdly, 98.5° requiring the person to be "warmed up" so as to be normal. Strict adherence to the *DSM-IV* criteria should not and cannot replace practitioners' careful and detailed clinical assessment. Clinical diagnoses are made by clinicians based on actual patient presentation and not on the abstract beliefs of a committee.

FRANK AND ERNEST reprinted by permission of Newspaper Enterprise Association, Inc.

Exhibit 6.1 presents the *DSM-IV* diagnostic criteria used for ADHD. There are essentially three types of ADHD: (a) the Combined Type exhibiting inattention, impulsivity, and hyperactivity (coded 314.01); (b) the Predominantly Inattentive Type in which the primary symptom cluster is inattention (also coded 314.00); and (c) the Predominantly Hyperactive–Impulsive Type (coded 314.01). Unfortunately, in *DSM-IV* every diagnosis of ADHD is called "Attention-Deficit/Hyperactivity Disorder." Thus, an adult who has a hyperactive component would be officially diagnosed as "Attention-Deficit/Hyperactivity Disorder, Primarily Hyperactive–Impulsive Type." If the hyperactivity and impulsivity also had inattention, the person would be diagnosed as "Attention-Deficit/ Hyperactivity Disorder, Combined Type." If the patient does not have a hyperactive component, then he or she would still be diagnosed as "Attention-Deficit/Hyperactivity Disorder" with the modifier "Predominantly Inattentive Type." Although such nomenclature is difficult for patients, families, and employers to comprehend, it is the presently accepted medical nosology, at least until modifications are made in the *DSM-V.*

The *DSM-IV* diagnostic criteria also permit the additional qualifier "In Partial Remission" for those individuals who have some symptoms but who no longer meet the full criteria. Generally, this means that the individual had blatant and full-blown symptoms as a child or adolescent, but having matured in chronological age and experience, some of the symptoms have remitted or are under better control. Thus, the qualifier is added to reflect that state.

Very often clinicians find that some individuals who have demonstrable attention deficits do not fit these criteria. In such instances, it is entirely appropriate to use the category of "Attention-Deficit/Hyperactivity Disorder, Not Otherwise Specified" to capture those *DSM-IV* "atypical" presentations. This also allows for some of the wide variations seen in some patients with ADHD.

Case Vignette: Phil

Phil, age 43, is married to a secretary-receptionist for a local law firm. Their three children are ages 5, 3, and 1, reflecting delayed childbearing for the couple. Phil quit school in the 10th grade and went to work on a production line making tin cans. Over the years he was promoted to foreman. The noise of the can factory was such that, unless one was shouting in someone's ear, one could not be heard. Very little socializing went on during the shift. Phil's supervisory responsibilities were carried out by posting assignments rather than by interacting directly with other workers.

His wife had convinced Phil to see a therapist because she was "tired of being embarrassed by him." At home he was a good father to the three children, but socially, with friends or at her office parties, he would blurt out inappropriate comments and misread what other people were saying to him. He lacked the skill to read social cues.

His history indicated a disruptive school-age person; Phil described the principal as his "best friend," because he was in the office so often. His peers tolerated him and would say that "Phil the pill" was just being himself. Phil was not strong academically but learned readily from experience.

Phil had ADHD but with few symptoms, mainly blurting out, making social blunders, and failing to read social context and cues. The diagnosis was ADHD Not Otherwise Specified. Treatment consisted of regular attendance at support groups, group therapy for adults with a similar lack of social skills, and social rehearsing with role playing, which improved Phil's social life and reduced his wife's embarrassment.

Modifying Criteria for Adults

USING THE CRITERIA

In going through the *DSM-IV* criteria (see Exhibit 6.1), clinicians will note that some of the criteria are not oriented to adults, and they may want to phrase questions in this area to reflect more adult behaviors. Probing for behavioral symptoms of ADHD varies with each patient; some endorsements are easier to obtain than others.

In reviewing criterion A1a, fails to give close attention to details, clinicians should determine if the patient has difficulty with tasks requiring detailed and tedious work such as doing spreadsheets, preparing income tax forms, doing research, and typing. Detailed work is often very stressful for adults with ADHD; they also easily forget where they put things.

For criterion A1b, has difficulty sustaining attention, clinicians should inquire into problems with attention in leisure time and in work activities. Clinicians may wish to probe whether a patient is able to stick to a task until it is done or the extent to which his or her mind wanders until he or she loses track of what is being said or discussed. Clinicians can ask how easily or quickly a patient becomes bored and how often he or she seems to crave novelty. Does the individual find routine tasks problematic and thus procrastinates in doing things until the last moment?

Behavior to probe for under criterion A1c, does not seem to listen, include the adult's inability to listen when being spoken to, difficulty in paying attention to conversations, or forgetting what he or she heard and, therefore, not following the conversation. Often colleagues complain that the person is "tuned out" of verbal exchanges.

For criterion A1d, does not follow through on instructions, clinicians should focus queries around the patient's ability to complete projects that he or she has begun or to complete tasks and meet deadlines.

Under criterion A1e, problems related to day-to-day organization, information can be gleaned by asking whether the patient often experiences feelings of being overwhelmed or even paralyzed by multistep projects or those with several intermediate goals along the way. Does he or she lose track not only of work plans but also of personal and family plans as well, such as when or where the patient or the family needs to be at a particular moment in time? Does the patient have problems paying his or her personal bills on time?

Criterion A1f, difficulty with sustained mental effort, sometimes can be discerned by asking how many "piles of stuff" the patient has in different parts of the home (dining room table, desk, kitchen counter) as well as in the office. Adding questions about paperwork or repetitive work activities also may be helpful in teasing out problems with sustained inattention. Does he or she find desk jobs or repetitive work more of a problem than constantly changing job activities?

For criterion A1g, the everyday tasks necessary for job completion are a good place to investigate this symptom. Does the sales person misplace product samples, order blanks, and so forth? A common problem of most adults with ADHD is frequently misplacing car keys.

For criterion A1h, note how easily the adult is distracted by extraneous stimuli, particularly in social situations. The patient attempts to listen to one conversation but is being drawn by the sound of other conversations; consequently, he or she is unable to stay focused on the conversation that he or she is actually involved in. The adult with ADHD can find it difficult to drive a vehicle and carry on a conversation at the same time. Because he or she is easily distracted and unable to focus, the driver who often fades in and out of conversations also tends to be an inattentive and potentially risky driver.

Criterion A1i, forgetful in daily activities, is related to A1g. The aim is to focus on forgotten activities such as keeping appointments, attending meetings, completing paperwork, picking up the children, getting a few grocery items, and so forth.

Under the Hyperactivity criteria, for criterion A2a clinicians can ask questions about fidgetiness and restlessness at one's desk or work station. Such individuals may need to have something in their hands to play with, may knock their knees, or may tap their toes.

For criterion A2b, is the adult "compelled" or feel a strong need to get up from the desk or work station? Does he or she frequently get up to get a cup of coffee or talk with a coworker? Patients will readily admit that they can sit only for a few minutes before feeling ready to "bust" if they do not get up and walk around every 20 to 30 minutes.

In criterion A2c, the feeling of restlessness may be manifested in the unconscious playing with objects on the desk or even absent-mindedly breaking pencils and tearing up sheets of paper.

For criterion A2d, clinicians should inquire about leisure time activities and how others react to him or her in social interactions. Do others express annoyance or complain about the patient's behavior? For example, friends may not want to go hunting, fishing, or watch movies with the individual because of his or her inability to stay quiet.

For criterion A2e, is often "on the go," clinicians again should be mindful of the subjective feeling of tension, stress, or anxiety if the person must remain stationary for some time (e.g., remaining seated). The constant need to get up and move regardless of the situation and its importance are relevant considerations. Criterion A2e also is relevant for adult patients in the work environment where they may become overcommitted and overscheduled.

With criterion A2f, does the patient talk excessively, constantly chattering and rambling, particularly in social situations? Does the patient lose track of the issue being discussed? During the clinical interview, a simple question may elicit a long-winded answer from the patient, and the clinician often may need to refocus the individual. Some patients' responses are tangential to the clinician's question, but if the clinician waits long enough, most patients will come back to and answer the question. Other patients may quickly realize their incessant verbalizing and admit with frustration that it happens often.

With criterion A2g, the patient is prone to making social blunders. The individual impulsively blurts out inappropriate comments in social situations, without thinking through the consequences of his or her actions. He or she makes premature or irrelevant remarks at inappropriate points of the conversation, such that colleagues perceive him or her as tactless, blunt, or unable to grasp the point being made.

Criterion A2h, difficulty in awaiting one's turn, is reflected in one's behavior in situations where queuing is necessary. Some adults with ADHD cannot stand in line. They will pace, rock, wiggle, and shuffle, frequently complaining that the line is moving too slowly.

Criterion A2i is related to A2g. The patient regularly interrupts other people's conversations without listening to what has been said or having no idea about the content of the discussion. Thus, probing for behavior that results in social blunders for the patient at parties or work gatherings is a relevant point of inquiry.

As stated in previous chapters, asking the patient how significant others (spouse, friends, coworkers, employer, children) would describe him or her can be a powerful projective technique. Follow-up questions should focus on others' perceptions of the patient's attention, concentration, distractibility, and hyperactivity levels.

DISTINGUISHING DIAGNOSIS VERSUS ASSESSMENT

A distinction needs to be made between the basic diagnosis itself and potential additional assessment. Often, extensive psychological assessment is not instructive in making the ADHD diagnosis. However, it may be necessary to clarify questions about underlying comorbid conditions. If a comorbid disorder is found, it may be integrated into the overall treatment plan. The treatment plan may include additional psychotherapeutic work but may affect psychopharmacological treatment as well, as in the presence of underlying depression. Furthermore, follow-up assessment may include a possible LD. A finding of LD may be useful information in guiding the patient toward more realistic and appropriate career choices. These evaluations also may be instructive in formulating additional components to a treatment plan, such as tutoring or educational support on the job or at school.

Medication Management and Referral

Because pharmacological management is often a component of a multifaceted treatment program for ADHD, it should be considered with every adult with ADHD. Medication can make a significant impact on the individual's overall functioning by reducing the severity of some of the ADHD symptoms and by contributing to the success of other interventions.

There are instances in which the need for referral to a physician for medication evaluation and management is necessary, but the patient may not be interested in pursuing a pharmacological modality at that point in the treatment process. Many misperceptions exist regarding medication management, such as the myth that stimulants do not work for adults and the belief that prolonged use of stimulants leads to addiction (these issues are discussed in detail in chapter 7). Practitioners are better able to help patients in making a decision regarding whether to include medication in their treatment if they initially explain the benefits and side effects. On occasion, I have recommended a book on the topic—such as Garber, Garber, and Spizman (1996); Hallowell and Ratey (1994); or Wender (1995)—to increase a patient's awareness and understanding.

Work with adults with ADHD will regularly require close collaborative relationships with physicians. Most patients will want a copy of the psychological evaluations sent to their primary care physician. In establishing collaboration, practitioners should provide some basic evaluation information in writing. When medication is indicated, clinicians should inform the physician in a general way that pharmacotherapy has been discussed with the patient and indicate the patient's preferred course of action. If the patient is not ready to commit to pharmacotherapy for the moment, practitioners can advise the physician that such treatment can be reintroduced at a later date.

Practitioners should not lose sight of the fact that they are the principal providers of overall behavioral management and care for the patient and that physicians providing medication management are consultants. (Chapter 7 discusses this point in greater detail.) The therapist's responsibility should be clearly articulated to both patient and physician. Treating adults with ADHD is usually a multimodal treatment plan. Most primary care physicians are more than happy to provide the pharmacological management and leave the behavioral intervention related to home, interpersonal, work, career, and life issues to mental health practitioners. It is likewise the responsibility of clinicians to determine and establish additional collaboration with other professionals, such as college placement officers, tutors, career assessment counselors, lawyers (for accommodations or job issues under the Americans with Disabilities Act of 1990), and so forth, as needed in the course of treatment.

Reimbursement and Billing Codes

ADHD is an accepted diagnosis by most in the health insurance industry, regardless of the nature of the plan. Most plans will permit a psychiatric diagnostic examination (procedure code 90801) and 1 to 2 hours of additional psychological assessment (96100) or neuropsychological assessment (96117). Supporting the diagnosis by describing symptoms around the presence of the four core symptoms (distractibility, impulsivity, inattention, and with or without hyperactivity) in operational terms is most acceptable to health insurers. For example, on one of these initial insurance forms, a patient was described as having significant job-related problems, as the patient has regularly missed deadlines due to his problems in organization and inattention. The patient becomes more stressed and dysphoric because of his forgetfulness. The person also has a history of impatience and angry outbursts with both his spouse and children.

Some insurers will require written feedback following the initial evaluation if the clinician plans to do any ongoing work.

With managed care organizations the problem-focused descriptors will not only facilitate the authorization of additional care; it is frequently the appropriate level of care for the adult with ADHD with no comorbidity or whose comorbid problems are not presently being addressed. The focus of treatment in this instance is helping the patient understand the expression of the ADHD symptoms and how to make the world more ADHD supportive. I have never had any insurance reimbursement plan deny ongoing care for an adult with ADHD; other practitioners that I informally surveyed reported similar experiences. Insurance plans will usually reimburse ongoing care lasting several months to over a year as additional psychological problems and issues are uncovered.

When a third-party payer mandates more detailed information, the practitioner should review the ongoing treatment and future plans with the patient and discuss the written information to be sent to the health insurer. This joint discussion reviews and clarifies the treatment plan, confirms the patient's concurrence with the plan, and ensures that the patient understands and agrees to the kind of information being recorded for insurance purposes and that the patient is comfortable in having this information released. Rarely have I been asked by a patient not to forward the treatment plan to an insurance carrier. In those few instances in which the patient did not want the insurance carrier billed, he or she preferred to pay for services out of pocket.

The health insurance industry is becoming increasingly aware of the presence of ADHD in adulthood. The impact on the quality of life of the patient and the costs of not treating ADHD are compelling arguments to the insurer. It has been my experience that if treatment follows diagnosis, the insurance payers have not presented problems or additional obstacles. Unfortunately, the amount of paperwork required for reimbursement is not reduced.

Occasionally, the ADHD diagnosis that was initially correct will change with treatment. For instance, anhedonia may have been initially associated with ADHD but, in the course of treatment, the real mood problem is found to be depression and not just anhedonia. The rationale for the change in diagnosis and treatment should be clearly written and documented, along with whatever additional information is collected. If this is done, the change in diagnosis and treatment should not pose any problems for treatment authorization or for reimbursement. The practice of changing diagnosis and treatment plans in light of new information is well accepted by the insurance industry.

Conclusion

Once the ADHD diagnosis is made and a multimodal treatment plan is determined, psychological and pharmacological interventions affecting the patient's behavior at home, at work, and toward his or her overall environment should be consistent with the diagnosis. Practitioners should not anticipate problems or difficulties with health insurance companies. In fact, one advantage of working with adults with ADHD is that they can be quite vocal in their needs and will not take lightly an insurance denial of care for a disorder that has seriously hampered the quality of their lives for a very long time.

References and Resources

American Psychiatric Association. (1994). *Diagnostic and statistical manual of mental disorders* (4th ed.). Washington, DC: Author.

Americans with Disabilities Act of 1990, Pub. L. 101-336, 104 Stat. 337.

Cook, J. (1997). *The book of positive quotations.* Minneapolis, MN: Fairview Press.

Garber, S. W., Garber, M. D., & Spizman, R. F. (1996). *Beyond Ritalin.* New York: Villard.

Hallowell, E. M., & Ratey, J. J. (1994). *Driven to distraction.* New York: Simon & Schuster.

Wender, P. H. (1995). *Attention-deficit-hyperactivity disorders in adulthood.* New York: Oxford University Press.

Treatment Menu   7

We didn't possibly know where it would lead, but we knew it had
to be done.

—Betty Friedan

There is no cure for ADHD. The goal of treatment is to help the individual
understand, control, and manage his or her ADHD and modify the environment to adapt to behavioral problems. Usually, the main components of treatment are education, medication, psychotherapy, and environmental modification. The basic treatment paradigm for adults with
ADHD is intervention when and where their symptoms affect or interfere with any facet of their lives. Because of the nature of ADHD, treatment is both short and long term. The latter more often is episodic over
the life course. Over the years, the adult with ADHD may require a
variety of pharmacological, psychotherapeutic, behavioral, and environmental management interventions. The menu of interventions used by
the practitioner depends on patient presentation and issues. Treatment
goals and objectives will most likely change over time.

Patient Education

An initial and ongoing treatment consideration with adults with ADHD
is the need for providing current and updated education about this disorder. Research in this area is expanding rapidly, and individuals experiencing ADHD-like symptoms may hear or read about adult ADHD
and seek psychological consultation to determine whether they have

this problem. As more people learn about adult ADHD, various treatment fads that generally have no demonstrated effectiveness inevitably arise, about which patients will often ask the practitioner. Therefore, the first treatment guideline is actually one for practitioners: Be well informed and current in the knowledge of ADHD so as to adequately educate patients.

Educating adults with ADHD about their condition should include the latest information available regarding each patient's diagnosis, treatment, prognosis, and outcome. Patients should be educated not only about the facts but also about the myths that have evolved about ADHD.

Following the diagnosis, clinicians should start by telling patients about the signs and symptoms of ADHD and how the type, patterns, and intensity of these symptoms differ among individuals. Without delving into detail on neurological and neuropsychological functioning, practitioners should inform their patients that ADHD might involve a neurochemical disorder primarily affecting brain activity and arousal. Many researchers believe that the culprit is the chemical transmitter dopamine. Individuals with ADHD appear to lack adequate amounts of dopamine in the synapse (presynaptic cleft) of the prefrontal area of the brain. They experience a rapid depletion of this synaptic transmitter, such that their arousal systems are poorly regulated (i.e., their nervous systems are underaroused). This portion of the brain is commonly referred to as the "executive" of the personality. The frontal lobes are responsible for maintaining appropriate focus and sequencing of events toward a specific goal. When the prefrontal lobe area is underaroused, individuals experience problems of impulsivity, goal directiveness, attention, and cognitive functioning. Thus, individuals with ADHD often have normal to above-normal intelligence but have significant defects in the executive functioning of their prefrontal lobes, causing inappropriate behavioral and cognitive responses.

Clinicians should educate newly diagnosed adults with ADHD about the four core symptoms of inattention, distractibility, impulsivity, and (with or without) hyperactivity. Patients should be helped to understand that although ADHD is not a blatant psychiatric or psychological disorder, it is a chronic disorder that could significantly affect one's quality of life in virtually every domain. Clinicians can illustrate specific ADHD symptoms by drawing from actual examples from the patient's history.

Patients should be told that ADHD runs in families, and the majority of individuals with attention deficits are born with the disorder. The disorder was not the result of poor parenting, bad diet, bad teachers or employers, or a marriage or any other social relationship.

To the extent it can be determined from the evaluation, clinicians should explain why the disorder was not diagnosed earlier. Various factors could explain why ADHD was not diagnosed in childhood, such as the fact that the ADHD nomenclature did not exist until 1980 *(DSM-III),* when it was initially used to describe behavior, and because the latitude of tolerance for ADHD-like behavior varies considerably in different cultures and environments. For example, some parents and teachers have high thresholds for tolerance of ADHD symptoms and, therefore, they do not see such behavior as problematic or they do not recognize them for what they are. Sometimes, ADHD symptoms are masked by a child's superior cognitive abilities, or children with high intelligence may learn on their own to compensate for their ADHD symptoms. These children often can be identified as oppositional or defiant, or they might have been viewed as just not working up to potential. They may also have been described as mentally lazy or underachieving. These and similar explanations will provide patients with the proper context for why the disorder was not diagnosed earlier.

Clinicians should emphasize that there is no adult onset of ADHD; it is a chronic, lifelong problem recognized only in recent years. Although currently there is no known cure for ADHD, medication usually can help control or suppress the symptoms. The practitioner should then outline proposed treatment, its various components, the duration of treatment, and how patient and practitioner evaluate progress.

Treatment is based on an individual review of when, where, and how the symptoms interfere in individuals' lives and subsequently applying appropriate interventions. Clinicians should explain that most individuals, even those without ADHD, exhibit some ADHD-like symptoms in the course of their daily activities. Such problems are diagnosed as ADHD depending on the degree, frequency, and the extent to which such symptoms negatively and significantly affect day-to-day activities. Clinicians should tell patients that no one exhibits all ADHD symptoms all of the time any more than anyone is depressed all of the time. There are days and times when an individual's focus and attention is better than others. Adults with ADHD should be assured that a number of interventions could be utilized to improve the quality of their lives. Therapists should be prepared to deal with any anger and despair that may surface after this diagnosis is made.

These basic facts about the genetic basis, symptomatology, and treatment of ADHD are important for newly diagnosed adults to understand, so that they can begin to alter their preconceived notions of themselves as being lazy, stupid, inept, bad, and so forth. If comorbid symptoms are diagnosed, these conditions also should be carefully explained. All of this information should be communicated at a level appropriate to each patient's education and background, and it should be presented at a pace that allows the patient to comfortably absorb and digest the information.

FRANK AND ERNEST reprinted by permission of Newspaper Enterprise Association, Inc.

SIGNIFICANT OTHERS

After the ADHD diagnosis has been made, it is often helpful to bring the patient and spouse (or significant other) for marital or couples therapy as soon as possible. Particularly at the beginning of treatment, helping spouses understand not only the nature of the disorder but also the reasons behind the patient's problematic behavior with or toward the spouse and family may lower the couple's marital tensions dramatically. The couple may realize that their problem is much like what Charlie, age 27 and married, said: "I live my life in boxes stacked one on top of the other, and there are no doors that connect the boxes." Charlie was referring to his emotions: At one point, he suddenly exploded in anger; the next instant, he had quickly simmered down, left that "box," and wanted to cuddle with his wife Carolyn. She, on the other hand, was puzzled, hurt, frustrated, and resentful of her husband's explosive temper while he was in the other "box." Charlie's behavioral problems of hypersensitivity, quick temper, low self-esteem, anger, and grief all had to be discussed in couples therapy.

Helping partners also understand the tendency of adults with ADHD to externalize blame for unfinished or incomplete tasks may help lower stress levels in the family. Providing partners with reading material on ADHD is also beneficial.

BIBLIOTHERAPY AND SUPPORT GROUPS

As part of the "immediate" treatment plan for adults with ADHD, the practitioner should provide the patient with appropriate bibliotherapy and information about ADHD support groups. A variety of educational and self-help books are presently available (see the Appendix). Clinicians can also provide information about local chapters of the National Attention Deficit Disorder Association and the Children and Adults with Attention Deficit Disorder (see the Appendix), as well as their respective national organizations. The local chapters provide the active support group network, and the national organizations provide information through their regular in-house publications on issues relevant to ADHD in adulthood. If patients have Internet access, informational Web sites and ADHD chat rooms can be helpful as well (see the Appendix). This information is valuable and therapeutic for patients because it empowers them to take some personal control over the disorder and makes them aware that many others share their problem.

The importance of support groups cannot be overemphasized; they are upbeat and positive in outlook. There are discussion groups that focus on intervention strategies. Some groups invite guest speakers. Support groups are places in which to pick up information on new treatments and on professionals providing treatment. Most important, they are places where adults with ADHD will not feel alone and isolated (see the Appendix).

Recently, at one such group I attended, an adult with ADHD said that he could never find his car keys in the morning. Another participant asked if he had tried putting them on the kitchen table. He said that that did not work, as he did not always eat breakfast. Another suggested hanging the car key on a hook by the back door. He had tried that too, and that also did not work. A woman in the group asked if he had a garage and if it locked. The answer was yes. Then, the woman suggested, why not leave the keys in the car? He thought that was a great idea.

THATCH by Jeff Shesol

Medication

When medication issues are raised, in general, individuals with ADHD have one of two reactions. One group views medication as the "silver bullet" for all of their behavioral and interpersonal relationship problems. The other group absolutely refuses the idea of medication, as they equate it with illness, disease, or an inability to be in control. This latter group views medication as a "chemical straitjacket" that they fear will alter their personality. The fact is that pharmacotherapy is not an isolated treatment strategy, but rather a significant component of a multifaceted treatment plan used to control a neurobiological behavior problem. Medication is merely a tool, albeit a powerful one, that complements other treatments. Its use as part of a treatment plan for an individual with ADHD must always be carefully considered.

EFFICACY

Medication for ADHD normalizes the underarousal of the frontal lobe and permits some increased inhibition of the problem behavior, but additional interventions are also necessary. ADHD medications are remarkably successful in increasing attention and decreasing distractibility, impulsivity, and restless motor activity. Temper outbursts, emotional lability, and moodiness may be controlled, and problems with disorganization and forgetfulness may be improved. The extent of the improvement is variable, as it is not only dose related, but also varies from person to person. As long as the ADHD medication is in the bloodstream at therapeutic levels, improvement of some symptoms can be expected, although symptoms may recur when the medication wears off.

However, medication is not equally effective for all individuals and, although it will address certain symptoms, it does not necessarily control or inhibit all of the problematic behaviors. Patients need to understand that pharmacological agents will not improve their knowledge base or academic skills, although medication may permit them to learn more rapidly. Furthermore, medication will not help patients deal with their self-esteem or interpersonal interaction problems.

The efficacy of ADHD medication has been demonstrated in several well-controlled studies (Spencer et al., 1995; Bhandary et al., 1997; Wilens et al., 1998), but I am unaware of completed studies on definitive long-term effects of taking these drugs. However, the stimulants, and some of the antidepressants, have been used for years, and I have not heard of any anecdotal reports of long-term negative side effects. When I was the director of an attention deficit disorders clinic, we followed children and adolescents who were on such medication for several years without encountering a single incident or problem related to long-term use.

TYPES OF PHARMACOLOGICAL AGENTS

Table 7.1 is a list of the two classes of medication frequently used in the treatment of adults with ADHD. Table 7.2 describes common side effects by class of medication and how to deal with them.

TABLE 7.1

Medications Frequently Used in the Treatment of ADHD in Adults

Name	Dose available (range)	Onset/Duration
Stimulants		
Methylphenidate (Ritalin)	5, 10, 20 mg tablets (5–120 mg/day)	20 minutes, lasts 3–5 hours
(Ritalin SR)	20 mg sustained release (20–120 mg/day)	45–60 minutes, lasts 6–8 hours
Dextroamphetamine	5 mg tablets (2.5–40 mg/day)	20–30 minutes, lasts 3–5 hours
Dexedrine spansules	5, 10, 15 mg capsules (5–40 mg/day)	60 minutes, lasts 6–10 hours
Adderal (no generic)	10, 20, 30 mg (5–40 mg/day)	30–60 minutes, lasts 6–12 hours
Methamphetamine (Desoxyn)	5, 10, 15 mg tablets (5–45 mg/day)	30–60 minutes, lasts 6–12 hours
Pemoline (Cylert)	18.75, 37.5, 75 mg (18.75–122.5 mg/day)	lasts 12–24 hours[a]
Antidepressants		
Imipramine (Tofranil)	10, 25, 50 mg tablets (25–200 mg/day)	12–24 hours[a]
Desipramine (Nopramin)	10, 25, 50, 75 mg tablets (25–200 mg/dy)	12–24 hours[a]
Fluoxetine (Prozac)	10, 20 mg (10–40 mg/day) liquid 20 mg/5 ml (10–60 mg/day)	2–4 weeks, half-life several days
Sertraline (Zoloft)	50, 100 mg tablets (50–200 mg/day)	2–3 weeks, half-life 24 hours
Paroxetine (Paxil)	20, 30 mg tablets (10–40 mg/day)	2–3 weeks, half-life 14 hours
Burproprion (Wellbutrin)	75, 100 mg (100–450 mg/day)	3–4 weeks, doses 6 hours apart

[a]Takes several days to reach effective levels.

Note. From *Adolescents and ADD: Gaining the Advantage,* by P. Quinn (pp. 10–11), 1995, New York: Magination Press. Adapted with permission.

TABLE 7.2

Common Side Effects and Responses

Side effect	Response
Stimulants	
Appetite decrease/nausea	Take medication after meals with a full glass of juice or water; increase regular exercise
Stomach aches/headaches	Eat
Weight loss	Increase calories or add supplements
Insomnia	Decrease later doses; increase regular exercise
Irritability	Decrease caffeine intake; overlap doses if rebound phenomenon
Tics	Decrease dose; change medication
Depressed mood/social withdrawal	Re-evaluate medication and possible additional diagnosis
Antidepressants[a]	
Sedation/fatigue	Will gradually decrease over time; begin by taking medications at bedtime
Dry mouth/blurred vision	Drink plenty of liquids; chew gum, mints
Gastrointestinal distress	Take after meals; increase fiber
Nervousness/tremors/anxiety	Decrease dose; change medications
Mania/manic episodes	Discontinue
Insomnia	Decrease dose; change medications
Blurred vision	Observe; reduce dose if no remission

[a]Monitor cardiac status for tricyclics and liver functions for pemoline.

Note. From *Adolescents and ADD: Gaining the Advantage*, by P. Quinn (pp. 10–11), 1995, New York: Magination Press. Adapted with permission.

Stimulants

Generally speaking, in adults as in children, stimulants are the first line of pharmacological treatment. They are well tolerated by most adults. Although 70% to 80% of school-age children will respond positively to stimulant medication, the percentage drops somewhat to between 50% and 78% for adults (Wilens, Biederman, & Spencer, 1998). Gender, race, education, and family income do not predict response to stimulant medications.

In a recent review of the pharmacotherapy of adults with ADHD, Wilens et al. (1998) found no studies on the efficacy of the sustained release preparation of methylphenidate or dextroamphetamine. This does not mean that they are not used, but that their efficacy is anecdotal and experiential rather than documented by published studies. In that review, the most commonly reported side effects are insomnia, edginess, diminished appetite, loss of weight, dysphoria, obsessiveness, tics, and headaches. No medication-induced psychosis has been reported when the stimulant is in the therapeutic range; no reports of stimulant abuse have been noted in controlled or retrospective studies of adults with ADHD. A dose-dependent response efficacy to stimulants was found in two studies, and a "robust" dosing of 1 mg per kg was more effective than lower doses of .7 mg per kg.

Dosages are adjusted to meet individual needs and circumstances through close cooperation and collaboration with the practitioner, the patient, and the prescribing professional. The dosage must be individually adjusted to each patient (Elia, Ambrosia, & Rappaport, 1999), as age, weight, level of hyperactivity, or blood level (plasma) concentrations of the medication predict effective dosage.

For adults with ADHD whose symptoms are pervasive and encumbering, daily dosage of medication is the required treatment strategy. Frequently, the adult with ADHD, his or her spouse, friends, and co-workers will note changes in some behaviors with medication. However, there are some adults with ADHD who do not want to perceive themselves as "dependent" on medication for their ADHD. These patients may minimize the severity of the symptoms and state that they only need it at work, in class, or for study. Their perceptions and judgment may not always be accurate; thus, if possible, confirmation of the patient's behavior and symptoms from others will be helpful. Undermedicating is a concern and works against the best interests of the patient. Rating scales and computer tests of attention, when appropriate, also may be used to evaluate the adequacy of medical dosage.

For some adults with ADHD, medication can be used sparingly. For example, I have had patients who take their medication only at particular periods of time when they feel that they need medication to cope with specific situations. One patient was a city planner who, following his promotion, only could find the time to do his paperwork some three days before project reports were due on July 1 and on January 2. He therefore took his stimulant medication in the 4 weeks preceding the projects' due dates; at other times of the year, he did not use his medication at all. Another patient takes his medication only at work: He has programmed his office computer so that the first item that appears on the monitor is "Have you taken your meds today?" Some college students, aware that standard doses of stimulants last about 4 hours, will frequently adjust taking their medication to meet their classroom and study habits.

Antidepressants

Antidepressants are effective with both children and adults with ADHD and may be the pharmacological treatment of choice when there is a comorbid finding of depression or anhedonia, when stimulants are ineffective, or when there are unpleasant side effects from stimulants. Antidepressants have the benefit of once-a-day dosing, preferably at bedtime. Overall, however, antidepressants are not as effective for many patients as are the stimulants. Most of the antidepressants currently being used to treat adults with ADHD are listed in Table 7.1, but currently, only desipramine, nortriptyline burproprion, and sertraline appear to be most efficacious. For fluoxetine and paroxetine, their efficacy thus far is based on anecdotal or open trial evidence.

Stimulants and antidepressants can be used simultaneously, as one will potentiate the action of the other. It is possible, therefore, to augment the effectiveness of a stimulant by introducing an antidepressant without increasing the dosage level of the stimulant (see Wilens et al., 1998, and Bhandary, Fernandez, Gregory, Tucker, & Masand, 1997, for further discussion).

Hypertensive Drugs

Some information exists on the use of antihypertensive medications (such as clonidine and tenex) for ADHD in children. These medications target impulsivity and elevated activity level problems, but they have no discernible impact on problems with inattention. I mention these drugs because they could be a treatment alternative if the first two options do not achieve positive results. But, of course, these drugs affect the patient's blood pressure. To my knowledge, there has been no systematic study to date of the effectiveness of hyperactive drugs on adults with ADHD.

SUBSTANCE ABUSE

An important concern for practitioners and prescribing providers is the potential for substance abuse among patients with ADHD on medication. Stimulants, for example, have fairly high street value. Among patients who have a cofinding of substance abuse, this cofinding may affect the patient's decision not to utilize a stimulant. But perhaps the concern about stimulant abuse is overblown; with appropriate monitoring, the potential for abuse should not present a significant problem. The stimulant pemoline is not abusable, and it has demonstrated success in treating adults with ADHD. Problems with efficacy and the extended time before therapeutic onset can be overcome by the use of higher doses and rapid upward adjustment of dose (Elia et al., 1999). However, there are some concerns about the long-term use of pemoline because of possible liver damage.

It is helpful to have a spouse or significant other accompany the patient to medication consultation appointments to obtain additional information on the patient's medication response, increase the patient's compliance, and lower the possibility of abuse. Treatment paradigms can be tailored to individual need and lifestyles.

WOMEN

With female patients about to begin a pharmacological trial, clinicians should be aware that ADHD symptoms become more severe in the premenstrual week, particularly if the women also have premenstrual syndrome (PMS). PMS symptoms appear to be more intense when combined with ADHD and, thus, the depression, irritability, and anxiety noted in this group is further exacerbated. ADHD symptoms that have been ameliorated also become exacerbated when PMS symptoms are present, and it may be necessary to either increase the pharmocotherapy for the ADHD or introduce an additional agent, such as Zoloft, to alleviate PMS symptoms. In addition, simply providing women with information on the interaction of ADHD and PMS is helpful, so that those experiencing both problems can prepare for extra-difficult days (Solden, 1995, p. 178).

MONITORING

It is important that the practitioner review with the patient the pharmacological component of the program. The practitioner will likely have repeated contact with the adult with ADHD, and checking dosage and frequency as taken versus as prescribed is a necessary component of all treatment. How and when the medication is taken can affect treatment, as well as the individual's behavior both at the workplace and at home. It is not unusual for patients to adjust their medications without informing the psychologist or the prescribing provider because they often are forgetful and disorganized. Their thinking is a bit like "I am taking one pill, and I feel a difference, so maybe two is better." Because response effectiveness is predicated on knowing how the medication is prescribed and taken, questions regarding compliance and dosing should be asked routinely by the practitioner, with feedback provided to the prescribing professional as necessary.

RESISTANCE

For individuals with ADHD who are disinclined to use medication as part of a treatment plan, their wishes should be respected if possible. In such instances, clinicians should move on to other interventions but also suggest reading material on ADHD and medication. As other courses of intervention proceed, the medication question may be revisited as necessary. Clinicians can advise the patient that in cases in which other treatment strategies are ineffective or are only minimally effective, medication could improve the outcomes. With children, behavioral and school-based interventions seem to work better with the concurrent use of medication; a similar combined treatment strategy will work for adults as well.

One effective strategy for those individuals who are unsure about taking medication or who would like a trial period is to devise a focused pharmacological trial with a prescribing colleague. The psychologist, in collaboration with the patient's primary physician, initially identifies certain difficulties that could be ameliorated by pharmacological management, such as increasing a patient's attentiveness to detail at work or attentiveness at business meetings. Because these medications tend to have a therapeutic window that varies from individual to individual, some titration of the medication may be necessary as part of this focused trial. The focused trial need not be included in the treatment plan eventually agreed to by the patient and psychologist.

PHYSICIAN–PSYCHOTHERAPIST INTERACTION

It is a nice touch to write a report in letter form to the patient's primary care physician or to whomever is following him or her for routine medical attention. Such a report also is necessary when a primary care physician refers a person to the clinician for an ADHD consultation.

In the letter, the evaluation is summarized, stating the patient's diagnosis and outlining the proposed treatment intervention. Toward the end of the report, the practitioner should indicate that he or she would be willing to follow the patient and work on his or her behavioral problems. Such a statement should be clearly articulated, particularly if the therapist is also requesting the physician to evaluate the patient for medication management. I regularly copy this letter to my patients, who use the letter as a springboard for follow-up care with me and as a reminder to make that appointment with the physician. In some cases, the letter triggers a response from a spouse or significant other to encourage the person to follow through on treatment.

Psychotherapy

A treatment menu would necessarily include individual psychotherapy to help patients with ADHD deal with personal, family, and work issues.

Long-term psychotherapy for ADHD alone is not warranted, except in complex cases in which comorbid conditions such as depression and anxiety exist and must be addressed concurrently with ADHD. Rarely is long-term psychotherapy for ADHD alone reimbursable by the vast majority of health insurers.

INDIVIDUAL PSYCHOTHERAPY

As with most patients, those with ADHD experience a temporary feeling of relief following diagnosis. However, shortly after, many patients begin to have difficulties with their diagnosis, not because they do not believe it, but because of the grief and the subsequent anger they feel due to lost opportunities and failed relationships. As one adult said, "I've got to stop cornering the market on being an asshole." Dealing with the initial anger and grief over the suffering that the patient went through for decades before the proper diagnosis was made is part of the therapy.

A caution should be made about the use of psychotherapy with adults with ADHD. Psychotherapy, although enormously helpful and useful, has the potential to be damaging as well. Because of the peculiarities of the ADHD symptomatology cluster, some deviation from the traditional patient–psychotherapist relationship may be necessary with this group of individuals. Adults with ADHD, as we know, often experience difficulties with follow-through. Forgetting is rampant, and many patients show up late for appointments (or at the wrong time or on the wrong day). Although there may be multiple reasons for these behaviors, the psychotherapist must keep in mind that these symptoms are usually caused by neurobiological problems characteristic of the ADHD cluster. Therapists need to exercise great caution, therefore, before assigning psychological or unconscious interpretations to these behaviors. These behaviors should not be interpreted in terms of transference issues, latent hostility, or passive–aggressiveness. To interpret these behaviors as "psychological" may well destroy the therapeutic alliance and contribute to the patient's negative self-perception.

In addition, many forms of individual psychotherapy rely on following patients' verbal and affective flow and, as such, the therapeutic sessions may be relatively unstructured and unguided. These techniques, although appropriate for many other individuals, tend to be ineffective with adults with ADHD. The lack of continuity in a free-flow psychotherapeutic session tends to be counterproductive. Such patients often need external organizers, reminders, and prompts. I have found it helpful to have patients keep a psychotherapy notebook and even take notes during sessions. At times, I suggest that patients write a reminder in the notebook, usually about something to consider and remember after the session. I also give patients homework assignments between sessions, and I have them enter these in their psychotherapy notebooks. At the beginning of a session, I review what the patient and I hope to accomplish that day in that session and, toward the end of the session, I discuss what was accomplished in the session. I frequently ask patients to write down what we will do next week as part of the homework assignment.

Another deviation from the traditional patient–therapist interaction is for the therapist to extend his or her assistance beyond the confines of the office, when necessary and appropriate, for the patient's well-being. For example, it may be necessary to call the patient's workplace to remind him or her of the next session. Some patients ask whether my office staff could do that, and some patients have requested that I advise their spouses of their next appointments. In one instance, a patient requested that I give his therapy appointment schedule to his employer, who was very supportive of his treatment efforts. In another case, I was asked to page a coworker of the patient at a specific time; the coworker would then call the office, and then the office would call the patient to remind him that his appointment was in an hour. This arrangement was very effective, and the individual never missed an appointment again.

OTHER FORMS OF PSYCHOTHERAPY

Marital therapy also can be used not only to educate the spouse or significant other, but also to rebuild and strengthen the couple's often fractured relationship. Living with a spouse with ADHD can be like living through an endless succession of social tornadoes and earthquakes.

Family therapy sessions with the whole nuclear family and with selected members of the extended family may be necessary and useful. Composition of the family therapy session will depend on which relationships are strained and, over time, various combinations of sessions with different family members could be arranged as relationships improve or deteriorate.

Group therapy also may be used as an adjunct treatment, or it may be used alone as the primary intervention. ADHD groups could assist patients with everyday social-skills problems, from behavior toward others at home to behavior on the sports field or in the local supermarket to behavior in the workplace. The group therapy situation also provides patients with a sense that they are "not totally different," that there are others like them. Group therapy also provides a forum for sharing and learning successful coping strategies.

There may also be a need at some point for focused psychoeducational therapy (and skills building) around anger control and stress reduction. Patients may need assistance in learning how to modify anger and emotional lability attached to specific affective issues or environmental events and also may need to learn, among other skills, such activities as progressive relaxation techniques to reduce stress.

Also, for most patients with ADHD, their organization and time management skills are almost always in need of amelioration. Disorganization is probably the most frequent complaint of adults with ADHD. This executive function is related to problems with memory, and a period of concentrating on techniques for enhancing memory, creating systems for self-reminding of needed actions, and undertaking similar skills building can be used.

All of these other forms of psychotherapy will not be typically provided immediately. However, because ADHD cannot be "cured" and the most typical treatment plan will involve different short-term interventions over time, many different interventions can be used with adults with ADHD, selecting whatever is most appropriate for the current problem or problems.

SCHOOL- AND WORK-RELATED INTERVENTIONS

Often adults with ADHD seek treatment because of school or job-related problems. The college student with ADHD will present with failing grades, or the employee with ADHD has difficulty keeping a job. One patient in my practice has held 30 jobs in as many years. His impulsivity usually got him fired or caused him to quit for reasons that he could not remember. Immediate intervention by the therapist may be necessary to restructure the school or work environment. Strategies may be simple or complex, from allowing the student more time on tests in a quiet room to arranging for the worker's desk to face the wall to applying the "reasonable accommodations" rule permitted under the Americans with Disabilities Act (ADA) of 1990.

For young adults with ADHD, issues to grapple with in psychotherapy involve career planning and choice of future employment, which requires the therapist to take on some of the roles of a vocational counselor. Frequently, extensive therapeutic work needs to be done on issues related to the patient's occupation and relationships with coworkers. Initially, the patient is faced with the dilemma of whether or not to divulge his ADHD at the workplace. If he or she chooses to do so, patient and therapist will need to explore the advantages and disadvantages of invoking his or her rights under the ADA and insisting on accommodations. The adult with ADHD must learn how to articulate his or her special needs at work and learn to negotiate how to get those needs met.

DEALING WITH STRESS

Stress and ADHD are like oil and water; they do not mix well. Individuals with ADHD are much more susceptible to the effects of stress than are individuals without ADHD. For most people, stress can be found in any segment of our lives, and we learn to cope in various ways. In the case of individuals with ADHD, stress can profoundly exacerbate ADHD symptoms. Thus, stress reduction is an important goal to begin to achieve right after a diagnosis. Stress relief is almost always a part of the initial treatment plan, and it will continue as new stressors are identified. One important task of therapists is to assist patients in working toward achieving a less stressful lifestyle by helping them take control of ADHD symptoms and behavior.

The psychotherapeutic sessions, therefore, should accomplish a variety of interventions, requiring active interaction with the patient, the family, the place of employment, and even the community. As the case manager for the patient's overall care, the practitioner must maintain regular contact with the prescribing professional (if the patient is on medication for ADHD), the school or workplace, the spouse and family and, in the case of comorbid conditions, with other health care professionals. This type and level of involvement outside of therapy with individuals other than the patient is atypical and potentially overwhelming for professionals who are unfamiliar with working with patients with ADHD. Much of this additional intervention is geared to assisting patients to create a less stressful environment.

Environmental Strategies

An important component of the treatment plan for adults with ADHD will necessarily focus on a review of needed environmental changes and adjustments that can reduce the expression of symptoms and their impact on the individual. The practitioner's task is teaching patients to understand what constitute an optimal environment and lifestyle for individuals with ADHD, helping them identify behavioral problem areas, and restructuring their current environment and lifestyle to minimize and control their disability. For example, the clinician may guide the patient in selecting the right college or graduate specialization, selecting a good job match, reducing stress, improving memory, and so forth. Patient and practitioner develop a therapeutic alliance to actively participate in the healing and change process.

Practitioners encourage patients to undertake a daily review of their routine: what is going well and what is not, what works and what does not. Many problems for adults with ADHD arise from their inability to stay organized and follow through despite their best intentions. For them the use of a professional organizer may be beneficial. Taking advantage of time management seminars or systems such as the Franklin

Planner or similar computer programs that help individuals bring organization to personal chaos are helpful. A "WatchMinder" wrist watch provides up to 60 vibrating reminders and can be set to vibrate at different times and display a message of what the person has to do at each time, such as "take meds," "doctor's appointment," and so forth (available from the ADD WareHouse; see the Appendix).

Neurobiofeedback

In the past few years, there has been a great deal of interest in neurobiofeedback or electroencephalogram training. Neurobiofeedback attempts to train the individual to increase the brain activity associated with paying attention while decreasing the brain activity associated with daydreaming or distraction. Electrodes are attached to the person's head to amplify the brain waves. The brain waves are transmitted to a computer, which translates the brain waves into a computer game. The person is taught how to manipulate brain activity by concentrating and manipulating the computer game. Neurobiofeedback has been tested as a treatment for migraines, stress, and high blood pressure, but research into its effect on ADHD has been limited to case studies tracking individual improvement (e.g., Gendar, 1996). Some case studies show initial promise. Full-scale, scientifically controlled studies have yet to be undertaken, but this appears to be a promising intervention.

Neurobiofeedback treatment of adults with ADHD is intensive (2–5 times per week). Numerous sessions are required for adults (25–40), and treatment is costly in the short run. However, treatment has the potential to be cost effective in the long run, as it may reduce or eliminate the need for medication, which may be more costly over several years. Proponents of neurobiofeedback are beginning to demonstrate the effectiveness of this treatment modality. Unfortunately, in 1997, the Technology Evaluation Center of the BlueCross BlueShield National Association reviewed over 30 studies of biofeedback and concluded that improved health outcomes have not yet been established (BlueCross BlueShield Association Technology Evaluation Center, 1997); therefore, this intervention is usually not covered by medical insurance. However, neurobiofeedback is an emerging treatment modality for ADHD patients, and the research in this area should be monitored.

Health Fads

There are currently many popular beliefs about particular foods causing ADHD and natural health foods purporting to alleviate or minimize symptoms. It is sometimes argued that sugar, for instance, causes ADHD and that removal of sugar from the diet will eliminate ADHD symptoms. Although ample literature exists to discredit this belief (Conners, 1980; National Advisory Committee on Hyperkinesis and Food Additives, 1980; Millich, Wolraich, & Lindgren, 1986; Wolraich, Wilson, & White, 1995), eliminating sugar from the diet continues to be a favorite home treatment, and patients frequently ask about its effectiveness. What the scientific evidence suggests is that, although dietary sugar intake may exacerbate certain ADHD symptoms in some people, it does not cause ADHD. This finding is clearer for children than it is for adults. Likewise, no scientific evidence exists showing that removing colors and additives from food has any palliative effect on ADHD.

Natural foods and supplements have become popular as treatment for all manners of maladies. I regularly receive material indicating how specific minerals, vitamins, spices, herbs, and combinations thereof have helped people with ADHD. The latest substance being mentioned as greatly aiding patients is pine tree sap. Vegetarian diets are no more helpful to adults with ADHD than high meat protein diets (but at least the vegetarian diet might lower serum cholesterol).

This literature, of course, makes no claim that these nutritional foods and supplements cure ADHD, but they do describe the "vast improvement" achieved as a result of taking them. Neither has any well-controlled research demonstrated that megavitamins or orthomolecular vitamin therapy proved effective in addressing any of the ADHD symptomatology. All supporting information for these claims is anecdotal or testimonial. No controlled crossover or double-blind research exists to date to suggest that such "natural" elements will significantly alter ADHD symptoms or behavior.

Also, there are isolated case reports, but no hard and compelling data, that vestibular treatments or inner-ear treatments have been helpful with individuals with ADHD. There is no solid evidence that optometric or visual training is a useful treatment intervention for adults with ADHD. Before these popular interventions can be taken seriously and included in the treatment armamentarium for adults with ADHD, rigorous scientific proof of their efficacy must be demonstrated over and above mere testimonials and a few case reports.

Conclusion

Although ADHD has no cure, an effective multifaceted treatment strategy exists to help the individual understand his or her ADHD-related problems, control and manage the symptoms, and help him or her lead a productive and satisfying life. The components of this treatment paradigm usually consist of education about the disorder, medication, psychotherapy focused on ADHD concomitants, and environmental modification.

Patient education is the core of successful treatment for ADHD, because patients need to be educated to accept and understand their condition. The basic facts about the genetic basis, symptomatology, and treatment of the disorder are important for patients to understand, so they can think of themselves in a new light and follow through with a multimodal treatment plan. In addition to printed literature, ADHD support groups can greatly enhance patients' knowledge and provide tremendous assistance and support.

Psychological management, along with patient education, are the key ingredients to successful drug treatment. Stimulants and antidepressants used to treat ADHD symptoms are remarkably successful in increasing attention, decreasing impulsivity and restless motor activity, and controlling temper outbursts and emotional lability. Because drug dosage and use must be carefully monitored, cooperative interaction between the therapist and the prescribing professional will be highly beneficial to the patient. Medication, however, is not equally effective for all adults with ADHD and, although medication can address certain symptoms, medications will not control or inhibit problem ADHD behaviors. Consequently, medication should not be the sole treatment for an adult with ADHD, but should be used to complement other treatments, such as psychotherapy and other psychosocial interventions. Neurobiofeedback may eliminate the need for medication management.

Psychotherapy is necessary to help patients deal with personal, family, interpersonal, and work problems that tend to develop because of ADHD-related behaviors. Often, the amount of psychotherapy needed will be brief but intermittent. Common types of psychotherapy generally used include individual, focused psychoeducational, marital, and group therapies. Practitioners, however, should be cautioned that because of the peculiarities of the ADHD symptomatology cluster, some modification and adjustments will need to be made to the traditional form of patient–psychotherapist relationship.

Finally, patients must learn to modify and restructure their environments, to the extent possible, to reduce the expression of ADHD symptoms. One of the practitioner's roles is to teach patients what constitutes an optimal environment and lifestyle. The practitioner helps the patient understand himself or herself and his or her values, talents, interests, and weaknesses and then guides the patient in finding or creating the appropriate social and physical environments in which he or she can best function.

Thus, an effective multimodal treatment strategy should not only help patients take charge of their ADHD problems, but also help instill hope, optimism, and encouragement that these adults can have better, more productive, and happier lives.

References and Resources

Americans with Disabilities Act of 1990, Pub. L. 101-336, 104 Stat. 337.

Bhandary, A. N., Fernandez, F., Gregory, R. J., Tucker, P., & Masand, P. (1997). Pharmacotherapy in adults with ADHD. *Psychiatric Annals, 27,* 545–555.

BlueCross BlueShield Association Technology Evaluation Center. (1997). Neurofeedback. *TEC Assessments, 12*(21), 1–13.

Children and Adults with Attention Deficit Disorders. (1997). *ADD and adults: Strategies for success from CHADD.* Plantation, FL: Author.

Conners, C. K. (1980). *Food additives and hyperactive children.* New York: Plenum.

Cook, J. (1997). *The book of positive quotations.* Minneapolis, MN: Fairview Press.

Elia, J., Ambrosia, P. J., & Rappaport, J. L. (1999). Treatment of attention-deficit-hyperactivity disorder. *New England Journal of Medicine, 340,* 780–788.

Gendar, A. (1996, April 11). Troubled students try biofeedback. *Journal News,* p. A1.

Linden, M., Habib, T., & Radojevic, V. (1996). A controlled study of the effects of EEG biofeedback on cognition and behavior of children with attention deficit disorder and learning disabilities. *Journal of Biofeedback and Self-Regulation, 21,* 35–40.

Millich, R., Wolraich, M., & Lindgren, S. (1986). Sugar and hyperactivity: A critical review of empirical findings. *Clinical Psychology Review, 6,* 493–513.

Murphy, K. R. (1998). Psychological counseling of adults with ADHD. In R. A. Barkley (Ed.), *Attention deficit hyperactivity disorder.* New York: Guilford Press.

Nadeau, K. G. (1995). *A comprehensive guide to attention deficit disorders in adults.* New York: Brunner/Mazel.

Nadeau, K. G. (1996). *Adventures in fast forward: Life, love, and work for the ADD adult.* New York: Brunner/Mazel.

National Advisory Committee on Hyperkinesis and Food Additives. (1980). [Report]. New York: Nutritional Foundation.

Quinn, P. (1995). *Adolescents and ADD: Gaining the advantage.* New York: Magination Press.

Solden, S. (1995). *Women with attention deficit disorder*. Grass Valley, CA: Underwood Books.

Spencer, S., Wilens, T., Biederman, J., Faraone, S., Ablon, S., Lapey, K. (1995). A double-blind crossover comparison of methylphenidate and placebo in adults with childhood-onset attention-deficit hyperactivity disorder. *Archives of General Psychiatry, 52*(6), 434–443.

Wilens, T. E., Biederman, J., & Spencer, T. J. (1998). Pharmacotherapy of attention deficit hyperactivity disorder in adults. *Disease Management, 9*, 347–356.

Wolraich, M. L., Wilson, D. B., & White, J. W. (1995). The effect of sugar on behavior or cognition in children: A meta-analysis. *Journal of the American Medical Association, 274*, 1617–1621.

Long-Term Treatment | 8

I have always wanted to be somebody, but I see now I should have been more specific.

—Lily Tomlin

The general treatment course for adults with attention deficits frequently involves intermittent interventions provided over the years as new issues and challenges occur. The ADHD symptom cluster is essentially stable, but the changing environmental demands of work and family on an individual's ADHD symptoms can vary over time. The clinician will likely have clusters of contacts with the adult patient with ADHD over a significant portion of the life span.

This chapter discusses the common problems and issues that adults with ADHD face in the course of their life for which they may need focused, short-term professional help. Life issues around marriage, parenting, career, and stress are potentially disruptive to the adult with ADHD. For all of these challenges (and others that are more idiosyncratic to a particular patient), individual therapy may be needed. Practitioners may serve as a couples therapist, family therapist, advocate, supporter, and coach at various points in the patient's life. In addition, patients should be aware that federal laws and regulations also exist to protect them from discrimination, including capricious termination by employers. Continuing collaboration and information sharing between clinician and patient is the model for clinical intervention with adults with ADHD.

Long-Term Issues

SELF-ESTEEM

Although self-esteem may initially seem an acute or immediate treatment goal, it frequently becomes a long-term goal as well. Poor self-esteem and learned helplessness are often the emotional by-products of recurring failure for adults with ADHD and must be part of long-term (although likely episodic) treatment.

Adults with ADHD frequently have a history of trying and failing or of being told repeatedly that they can do better but are basically lazy. Having tried unsuccessfully for years to live up to the expectations of parents, teachers, employers, and peers, they may at some point in their lives stop trying, a behavior which, unfortunately, merely reinforces the very problems that need therapeutic work.

Over the years I have seen many adults with ADHD with significant problems around learned helplessness. Unfortunately, the rigidity of their thinking and their hypersensitivity makes successful work in this area slow, tedious, and difficult. Nevertheless, this is an important aspect to explore with adults with ADHD. Energizing the "helpless individual" and helping him or her develop the confidence to try again is a significant step in empowering the adult to take more control of and actively engage his or her life situations.

I recently noted this helplessness and feeling of worthlessness in a 28-year-old man whose appointment with me was set up by his mother. He had a history of chronic academic underachievement despite his having solid intelligence and achievement tests scores. Procrastination and delay were his trademarks, he said. He had failed college twice. After a good start both times, he just stopped going to classes. He exhibited no signs of depression or drug history. He was just as confused about his behavior as was his family. By the time he reached college (and despite his initial excitement), the sense of helplessness and worthlessness that he had learned all through primary and secondary school haunted him. The descriptors used by his elementary school teachers (and him) were "unmotivated and underachieving." No one until now had ever asked why.

STRESS

Many of the stress-based issues and problems mentioned in the earlier chapters may resurface in the life of an individual with ADHD. I am reminded of one long-term patient, now in his mid-50s, who still seeks me out for episodic brief psychotherapy around specific life change issues. For many years, I had intermittently helped him with his marriage and parenting problems. More recently, he came to me to discuss issues about his possible early retirement and the impending marriage of his daughter. As he describes it, he comes in on occasion to "have my batteries charged" as he faces a new life challenge.

Debilitating stress continues to be one of the most common problems that adults with ADHD experience over the years. The source of the stress can emanate from any aspect of their lives—causing disorganization, chaos, impaired social functioning, and poor work performance. Major life events such as a move, a new job, the birth of a child, or the death of a parent or other family member could cause stress. Also, stress can be caused by something objectively minor, like picking up a car pool member or stopping at the store on the way home.

Altering one's routine, or even the repeated occurrence and build-up of seemingly minor stressful situations, can be fertile ground for ADHD-related stress. Minimizing stress is a cardinal rule for alleviating the symptoms of ADHD. Consequently, adults already stressed by their symptoms find coping even more difficult when additional stress places demands on an already overloaded system. Like an electrical outlet with too many connections to it, the addition of one more connection "blows" the circuit and shuts it down.

CHANGE

Significant changes in the life of an adult with ADHD can bring havoc. The change that can accompany new employment, a family move, or the loss of a loved one may cause an adult with ADHD to once again become hypersensitive to comments or criticisms regarding his or her behavior. Here the problem is not merely stress but a major change in the adult's life. This hypersensitivity can result again in rigid ways of thinking, giving rise to quick-tempered behavior, inability to see another's point of view, and misreading others' actions. Such unpredictable behavior requires active intervention, as marriages and employment can be jeopardized.

Often, it is the patient's spouse without ADHD who becomes aware of the changes in behavior, activity, and mood and who will encourage the individual to again seek a therapist. Problems may also develop at work, in relation, for instance, to job shifts and layoffs, career change, and retirement. However, employers, even when they know that an employee has ADHD, have difficulty understanding how they may react to such career changes. EAPs, for one reason or another, infrequently refer these employees for professional help. Because therapy at these times of uncertainty and added stress is recommended and helpful, the initiative for seeking help may have to come from other than the workplace.

INTIMATE AND MARITAL RELATIONSHIPS

Adults with ADHD who are in committed relationships often experience episodes of stress, dysphoria, and unhappiness. This places significant stress on the relationship. The partner who has ADHD may become reliant, almost dependent, on the partner without. At risk as well is the potential codependence of the partner without ADHD.

It is often helpful when the spouse is able to meet with the adult with ADHD in a session with the practitioner, because the practitioner can help explain, but not excuse, the various behaviors and peculiarities. Major issues that the practitioner must address with the couple include early contracting over the division of labor within the marriage; as the marriage matures, child rearing and increased responsibilities in the family and home need to be addressed. Marital and family problems are likely to develop, and the practitioner may have to deal with the fears and frustrations of the partner without ADHD, as well as helping him or her deal with the build-up of anger and resentment directed toward the partner with ADHD. In this situation, attention must be redirected toward the nonvolitional nature of ADHD behavior.

Partners without ADHD must be prepared to deal with the needs that some individuals with ADHD have for novel stimulation and excitement, as noted in chapter 3. The partner without ADHD, with guidance from the therapist, must be prepared to help his or her partner ward off or minimize the consequences of high-risk behaviors, as physical injury and financial loss are common outcomes.

Delegating household chores, budgeting, and paying bills may create problems for the couple. Couples therapy is often centered around facilitating the couple's ability to divide jobs and chores appropriately according to each partner's abilities and limitations. Because the partner with ADHD is likely to do poorly in routine, repetitive, and detailed tasks, such activities are better delegated to the partner without ADHD. Some marriages work very well in which the partner with ADHD receives what amounts to a weekly allowance, and all bills are paid by the partner without ADHD. In cases in which both partners have ADHD, more time is required to parcel out tasks that are appropriate for each adult while building in checks and balances to ensure that all tasks that need to be done are done in the appropriate time frame. Occasionally, one finds family arrangements in which a child without ADHD assumes the responsibility of making the family function when both parents have ADHD.

PARENTING

As discussed in chapter 2, it is clear that ADHD has a genetic component but is not gender linked. At least one-third of all men who had ADHD in their youth will have a child with ADHD. Identical twins share the trait, and first-born males are more likely to have ADHD than male or female siblings.

Individuals with ADHD may be reluctant to have children because they fear that their child also will have ADHD. Understandably, they do not want their child to suffer the years of anguish that they themselves experienced. They will recall, often with great pain, the feeling of being ostracized in the classroom, of being labeled a "slow learner" or a "space cadet," of being told that they were not working up to their potential, and of experiencing a lifetime of academic underachievement. Individual and marital therapy may be necessary to work through these fears. The practitioner can help allay fears by explaining to them that ADHD can be diagnosed very early in a child's development and that contemporary ADHD treatment is much more rigorous and comprehensive. There are also federal laws (discussed later in this chapter) that will provide for an appropriate education for a child with ADHD.

It also may be appropriate for the practitioner to discuss issues around spacing of children, so, given the probability of both children having ADHD, parents can plan to have them at different developmental stages. Couples may consider adopting a child, but adopted children tend to be overrepresented among children with ADHD. Should parents consider adoption, the practitioner should counsel them by providing information on what is known about adopted children and ADHD and by helping prospective parents ask the appropriate questions of themselves and of the adoption agencies.

Once the couple becomes a family, there may be times during their child's formative years in which therapy or parental guidance will be necessary to ensure consistent and meaningful interfamilial communication. Parents with ADHD need professional guidance as they prepare to talk to and counsel their child with ADHD. Adults can become more critical and more sensitive to the "embarrassing" behaviors of their children with ADHD because parents may see themselves in their children. This can have destructive consequences on the development of the child and the family unit. Treatment during these developmental years should focus on communication between the parents. Both need to problem solve and to be empathic and understanding with each other on issues about raising a child with ADHD and his or her siblings without ADHD.

Couples in which one or both parents have ADHD may need considerable help in developing appropriate child-rearing skills from the time of the birth through the time their young adult leaves home. Consistency in child-rearing patterns includes knowing what is appropriate and inappropriate behavior for a child with ADHD as well as for the sibling without. Parents need to learn the difference between an ADHD symptom such as "I can't stop wiggling my feet" versus oppositional or defiant behavior such as "I can't stop wiggling my feet, and I keep putting them on the table after I'm told to take them off the table." Oppositional and defiant behaviors need corrective consequences, whereas hyperactive behaviors do not. Because oppositional and defiant behaviors are significant comorbid findings in children with ADHD, these children are at risk of being abused. The risk is even greater if there is an impulsive and hyperactive adult in the family.

Parents may need help developing behavioral interventions for their children, such as setting up specifically tailored rewards and contingencies, because children with ADHD, like many adults with ADHD, do not respond to usual rewards and punishments. Also, the parents with ADHD may tend to overidentify with a child with ADHD and become overly permissive and tolerant—to the detriment of the child. Siblings without ADHD may suffer as well because of the parents' permissiveness and inconsistent follow-through.

WORK

Some minimal risk exists in informing one's employer about having ADHD, even after the employee is hired. People in general are not well informed about this disorder, and employers are usually only concerned with problems directly related to work output. As a general rule, the employee with ADHD should initially attempt to work out adjustments to accommodate his or her problem through informal channels. Only when this procedure fails and the employee's ADHD behavior results in risking job loss should the employee formally reveal his or her condition.

A technique that has met with some success is to have the employee with ADHD approach his or her employer with suggestions for solving his or her work-related problems. For example, one individual told his employer that he performed better when given written rather than verbal instructions and asked if his employer could either give him notes or send e-mails. The employer thought that this was a good idea and, in turn, he did it for everyone in the small manufacturing plant. Another patient, a secretary who shared a work area in what was called the "bull pen," informed her employer that the physical arrangement reduced her transcribing speed and accuracy. She explained that her speed and accuracy would improve if she could use part of an unused storage room as her office. Her employer thought that this request was a bit unusual but, as no one objected when her idea was posed to the group, her work

THATCH by Jeff Shesol

station was moved. Her transcribing speed and accuracy did, in fact, improve.

Case Vignette: Adrienne

Adrienne, age 38 and a primary care nurse, received high merit ratings and was soon promoted to charge nurse. After the promotion, she sought professional evaluation because of some interpersonal problems triggered by attention deficits. She sought treatment for the attention deficits, including medication, which she used only in social settings. When Adrienne's employer found out that she was taking ADHD medication from her responses to an annual self-reporting questionnaire, Adrienne was terminated, even though her ratings remained high. She did not take medication while on the job. She sought legal counsel and, with the judge's encouragement, she was reinstated. Few would argue that individuals with uncontrolled ADHD should not be employed in work settings in which attention deficits could lead to life-threatening errors. However, it is equally important to understand that a person's "disability" must be individually assessed for reasonable accommodations on the job.

Case Vignette: Allison

Allison, age 42, is a planner employed by a large municipal school system. She had been in treatment for several years for attention deficits. As she was promoted, although the overall quality of her work was adequate, her supervisors seemed less pleased with her performance. When things became intolerable for her, Allison informed her supervisors about her attention deficits and requested reasonable work accommodations to resolve her problems on the job. She wanted a larger computer screen so that more could be placed on the computer desktop at the same time and still be legible. She felt that she needed a new monitor with a larger screen because her present one was of poor quality and had small print such that she found her concentration wandering. Instead of accommodating her request, her employer indicated intent to terminate her employment.

Allison appealed that decision internally. Her therapist was called to provide testimony. The hearing officer (who was an official of the same school system) did not assign or find fault with either side but recommended a lateral move with some accommodations made. Allison was pleased with this outcome, as it removed her from her increasingly hostile and stressful environment while she still retained her job and her position on the career ladder.

In working with a person with ADHD seeking employment, the practitioner should provide the patient with some guidelines for suitable work criteria. As discussed earlier in chapter 3, people with ADHD are better suited for low-stress than for high-stress jobs, preferably in a distraction-free environment; for jobs with short-term goals and quick feedback; for jobs with a minimum of repetitive tasks; and for jobs with minimal paperwork. The individual with ADHD can handle long-term projects if these projects can be broken into a series of short-term discrete goals. Such projects also will require increased supervision. In addition, the preferred job for someone with ADHD is one that will permit regular breaks and movement without sacrificing performance.

Finally, adults with ADHD must be careful to avoid "rising to one's level of incompetence." For instance, an ADHD individual who works well as a sales person will not necessarily perform as well when promoted to a managerial position, because he or she may not be able to handle the additional paperwork entailed by the position.

Some individuals with ADHD may need to be referred to a vocational counselor. However, I have been impressed over the years with how many adults with ADHD have been able to self-select appropriate work environments. A recent example is a 25-year-old married man who lost his job as a printer's assistant. He decided to begin his own yard and grounds business. This fortuitous change removed him from a repetitive job and put him into a constantly changing outdoor environment. He is now building a successful small business.

WOMEN

At this time, data about attention deficits in women are somewhat limited. Women with ADHD have special medical and social concerns that can add additional stress to already stressful ADHD symptoms. Medical consensus strongly advises pregnant and nursing women to stay off of medication for ADHD-related symptoms, because pharmacological agents affect the development of the fetus, and they may be transferred to the newborn via the mother's milk. Thus, some women who are off medication during pregnancy or while nursing may need more regular therapeutic attention to restructure their home and work environments. For other women, being off medication during pregnancy may pose minimal problems because higher estrogen states during the pregnancy may reduce ADHD symptoms. The interaction of a woman's baseline symptoms, the effect of the pregnancy itself, and her environment will dictate changes in the treatment plan.

Women, in general, are more likely to be caretakers for invalid parents and spouses. Women, more often than men, will keep their ailing spouses out of nursing home or long-term care facilities and in the home. In addition, there are likely to be more women than men with ADHD who are single parents raising young children. Thus, the practitioner should periodically advise women of possible changes in their ADHD symptoms in the course of their life span, and every female patient, her family, and the therapist should be vigilant in noting these changes.

Interventions

MEDICATION MANAGEMENT

Life course changes may alter the effectiveness of the pharmacological treatment component, which needs periodic evaluation. I have seen adults whose medication program had not been re-evaluated in decades; one 30-year-old woman had not had her medication re-evaluated since she was 13. Significant changes during the course of life (such as returning to school, receiving a job promotion, moving and relocating, changing marital status, and so forth) frequently tax the individual's ability to focus and to attend to and tolerate stress.

A surprising number of adults with ADHD are unaware that these life changes contribute to increasing problems with ADHD. At different points in the patient's life it may be necessary for the therapist to coordinate the pharmacological needs of the patient with the prescribing professional, in addition to the therapist's regular clinical work directly with the patient.

It is important as well to review the medication treatment plan, as patients may not always take the drug as prescribed. Information on actual drug-taking behavior is helpful in assessing and determining with the patient the next steps in the treatment plan.

COMORBID CONDITIONS

Comorbid as well as transient medical problems can cause a variety of physical ailments, illnesses, or anomalies that negatively affect the individual's ability to cope with attention deficits. Any change in general medical status can impede the present coping strategies for the adult with ADHD. When the patient experiences comorbid medical problems, the therapist may once again need to work with the individual around such issues as stress that, up until now, had been well managed. Given that about half of all adults with ADHD will develop a chronic medical condition (in addition to chronic ADHD), the monitoring of general medical status is a significant component of the treatment plan over the years.

BIBLIOTHERAPY

As discussed in chapter 7, a practitioner should advise and encourage patients to use bibliotherapy and self-help groups. Both can be excellent complements to long-term treatment with a mental health professional. By connecting patients to both local and national ADHD support groups, they can develop long-lasting ties and friendships that can be a powerful adjunct to other treatments. In the months or years of contact that a practitioner has with a patient with ADHD, many new and appropriate print and electronic information will become available that the practitioner can recommend or provide. This ongoing conduit of information strengthens the therapeutic alliance and updates the patient's knowledge.

PROMPTS AND COACHING

Establishing and maintaining behavior patterns that are routine and predictable will greatly facilitate the life of an individual with ADHD. The ability to get and stay organized with the use of a variety of prompts mentioned earlier, such as small recording devices (e.g., a "Voice-It"), the Franklin Planner, self-adhesive notes, and a memo board, will help the individual with ADHD focus on immediate goals and tasks at hand. However, over an individual's lifetime, changes bring about new events, such as marriage, parenthood, job loss, and retirement. These events are likely to destabilize an adult's predictable environment. The practitioner's psychological services may be called on not only to stabilize the individual, but also to help the patient work through the attendant feelings of depression, isolation, inadequacy, and poor-self esteem. Indeed, in terms of long-term treatment, the therapist may, at times, function as a job counselor as patients try to adjust.

Coaching, as part of the treatment plan, has become increasingly popular with adults with ADHD. In general, the technique involves helping the person identify short-term and long-term goals in any realm of his or her life—work, school, relationships, and so forth. The therapist reminds the patient of the goals that he or she has set and the consequences of delay or wrong choices. The patient regularly checks in with the psychotherapist (daily, every other day, or weekly), usually by telephone and occasional face-to-face meetings. The patient informs the therapist what action he or she has taken or the progress that he or she has made toward the attainment of a specific goal. The therapist guides the patient and may suggest alternate routes to a goal, provide encouragement and reinforcement for appropriate action, or remind the patient of the consequence of inactivity or impulsive action.

Generally, only one or two goals can be worked on at a time. For example, recently I coached a former patient long distance. Having moved out of state, she could not find the time to find a physician to manage her medication. We set up a series of time-certain goals: First, call the local ADHD adult support group and get recommendations for a physician. Second, call and set up an appointment with the new physician. Third, request that all records from her previous physician be sent to her new physician. She was reluctant to do the latter, as she moved out of state without advising her prescribing physician and was "embarrassed." She tried unsuccessfully to manage on her own for a month without seeking professional assistance. After two weeks of my coaching her, with Monday, Wednesday, and Friday check-ins, she achieved all three goals.

ADVOCACY AND FEDERAL LAW

Intermittently, the practitioner may need to advocate for patients and teach them to advocate for themselves. On rare occasions, the practitioner might even be asked to testify as an expert witness for an employee with ADHD in both administrative hearings and in the courts.

Certain provisions in three federal laws exist to assist certain individuals, including those with ADHD, in educational and vocational settings depending on the age and circumstance. The first law is the Individuals with Disabilities Educational Act (IDEA, 1990), a reauthorization of legislation that mandates free and public education through secondary school or to age 21. Since 1992, ADHD has been identified as a handicapping condition under this law. Thus, young adults initially identified as having ADHD and who are still in high school may qualify for special education services.

Section 504 of the Rehabilitation Act of 1973 also has bearing on people with ADHD. Although this section is part of civil rights legislation, it mandates that all educational institutions, public or private, that receive federal funds make reasonable accommodations for an individual's disability that "substantially limits or restricts one or more major life activity." Although ADHD is not mentioned specifically, learning problems or disabilities are recognized as affecting one major life activity, namely, education. IDEA and Section 504 of the Rehabilitation Act are related, for although a student with ADHD in a public high school may not qualify for "special education," the student may qualify for services. Thus, instead of having an individualized education plan, the student can have an accommodation plan developed to address his or her learning problems caused by attention deficits. The student's school, family, and other relevant individuals generally work out what would constitute "reasonable accommodations" to benefit the student.

The third law that can assist adults with ADHD once they are out of school and in the workplace is the Americans with Disabilities Act (ADA) of 1990. This law extends the mandate under Section 504 of the Rehabilitation Act to private schools and businesses with 15 or more employees. The text is similar to the language of Section 504 in that a person's disability must place substantial limits or restrictions on his or her major life activity. ADHD places substantial restrictions on an individual's learning, interpersonal relationships, work, and concentration. In a recent federal memorandum (Agency for Health Care Policy and Research, 1999) to government reviewers, impaired concentration was specifically mentioned as a possible restriction on a major life activity. Thus, under this law, the employer must provide reasonable accommodations. However, it is also clear from the law that whatever the ADHD-related interfering problems may be, the person must be "otherwise qualified" to perform the job. That is, the person could be successful at a particular job if it were not for the ADHD interference.

The changing parameters of reasonable accommodation are frequently argued in and delineated by the courts. Some accommodations that have been used successfully for adults with ADHD have been modifying work schedules, working at home or having a home office, or making physical changes in the work environment (such as working in an office with no windows to avoid distraction or using a headset to block out environmental noise). There also can be modifications in workplace policies, such as taking notes or taping meetings or having orders "written" rather than given verbally. Relevant state laws regarding the workplace and disabilities may also exist.

Conclusion

ADHD has an unpredictable but chronic course. It is important for practitioners to anticipate their patients' potential ADHD-related problems so that patients can seek early treatment and thus increase the likelihood of achieving positive outcomes. Women with ADHD have gender-specific medical and social issues that can be added stressors. The stresses and strains for parents with ADHD are further magnified when children also have ADHD. In such instances, the burden of managing a household can be destructive to the point of breakdown or even suicide. As a patient with ADHD stated, "I live my life in piles. The piles are just moved from room to room, but they are never done." What the therapist must do for adults with ADHD is to reframe the past, restructure the present, and provide hope and aspirations for the future.

References and Resources

Agency for Health Care Policy and Research. (1999, August). *Diagnosis of attention-deficit/hyperactivity disorder* (Technical Review Number 3). Rockville, MD: Author. Retrieved April 5, 2000 from the World Wide Web: http://www.ahcpr.gov/clinic/adhdsutr.htm

Americans with Disabilities Act of 1990, Pub. L. 101-336, 104 Stat. 337.

Cook, J. (1997). *The book of positive quotes.* Minneapolis, MN: Fairview Press.

Gordon, M., & Murphy, K. R. (1998). Attention deficit/hyperactivity disorder. In M. Gordon & R. Keiser (Eds.), *Accommodations in higher education under the Americans With Disabilities Act: A no nonsense guide for clinicians, educators, administrators, and lawyers* (pp. 72–87). New York: Guilford Press.

Individuals with Disabilities Education Act, Pub. L. 101-476, 104 Stat. 1142 (1990).

Jackson, M. T. (1997). *The adult attention deficit disorders intervention manual.* Columbia, MD: Hawthorne Educational Services.

Latham, P. S., & Latham P. H. (1992). *Attention deficit disorder and the law: A guide for advocates.* Washington, DC: JKL Communications.

Nadeau, K. G. (1996). *ADD in the work place: Choices, changes and challenges.* New York: Brunner/Mazel.

Rehabilitation Act of 1973, Pub. L. 93-112, 87 Stat. 355, 29 U.S.C. 794.

Conclusion 9

It ain't over 'til it's over.
—Yogi Bera

Prevalence estimates for adult ADHD range from a low of 2% to a high of 10%. Based on various methodological approaches to estimating ADHD prevalence in adult life, the most reliable approximation is about 4%. This means that approximately 8 million U.S. adults experience debilitating attention deficits. Many adults are unaware that ADHD is a problem; these adults will usually attribute their behavioral problems to their being undermotivated, having below-average intelligence, or being helpless or worthless. Men are more likely to exhibit attention deficits than women, but this finding will likely change as diagnostic research tools and operational definitions are further refined.

Because of the prevalence of attention deficits in adults, ADHD should be part of every evaluation and consultation. ADHD should be a standard rule-out diagnosis. Initially, it may take effort to critically and accurately evaluate the four core symptoms of ADHD and their associated difficulties. Practitioners who work with behavioral disorders in childhood may find it easier to evaluate adults for potential attention deficits. However, with increasing contacts with adults with ADHD, training, and experience, practitioners can be equally sensitive to and adept at diagnosing ADHD behavior manifestations in adulthood. ADHD mimics many disorders, and several disorders mimic ADHD.

Practitioners should review carefully whether depression or dysthymia, anxiety, substance abuse, LD, or bipolar disorders are viable diagnoses. Careful interviewing and recognition by the practitioner of how ADHD symptoms express on the surface and where the symptoms differ from other similar disorders will help in making the appropriate differential diagnosis and treatment plan. Patients should be referred for specialized assessment when necessary and appropriate.

Treatment is usually, if not always, multifaceted. Treatment planning must include specific objectives that the patient can realistically attain, and the treatment plan must be continually reassessed. Pharmacotherapy as a part of treatment is often appropriate, as the evidence suggests that 50–80% of adults with ADHD will respond positively to stimulant medication. However, it also should be emphasized that pharmacological management is only one part of a multimodal treatment plan (and, in fact, manufacturers of medications used for ADHD clearly indicate this). As is the case with children, adults with ADHD do far better and have much better outcomes when treatment is multifaceted. Depending on the individual and his or her circumstances, there may be a need for ongoing individual, marital, or group therapy. In these instances, problem issues may be inner directed, socially directed, or interpersonally directed toward one's spouse or significant other. In addition, parenting and workplace concerns may be important foci of treatment as well. Recall also that there can be significant gender differences in patient presentation and treatment. These issues usually constitute the first wave of treatment interventions.

Education is a key ally with the adult with ADHD. Therefore, bibliotherapy is important. There are several books and articles that are directed toward understanding and treating ADHD in adulthood, which have proven positive value (see the Appendix). National organizations such as the Children and Adults with Attention Deficit Disorders (CHADD) and the National Attention Deficit Disorder Association (NADDA) are also good information and connecting resources for the ADHD adult. Most of these national groups sponsor annual meetings for professionals and ADHD adults and their spouses. These groups frequently have local chapters with local support groups that have been a facilitative influence on ADHD adults. These groups take a very positive and success-oriented approach toward treatment of ADHD, thus making them a good resource for social reports on how ADHD individuals manage and cope. In addition, the World Wide Web not only has sites for NADDA and CHADD, but also for other ADHD chat rooms and resources as well, such as those sponsored by the National Institutes of Health. The ability of these national organizations and bibliotherapy to empower ADHD adults is impressive.

For many adults with ADHD, there are intermittent as well as long-term interventions that require fine-tuning over the years. Treatment plans may need to be altered as the events in the environment or in life conditions change. The ADHD individual who marries or becomes a parent will often require additional treatment to help make the transition into these new areas of responsibility. Similarly, a move with or without a job change or a job change alone is also another area that may require additional intervention. At various times in the course of the ADHD adult's life, the therapist may have to function as an advocate, perhaps in the courts, on the job, or in family matters. Empowering patients to become self-advocates is an important component in people's daily functioning and is a major therapeutic goal.

The primary behavioral care clinician has overall case management responsibility for coordinating all components of the treatment plan, including collaborating with the prescribing physician and contacting employers and the courts when necessary. As there are short-term, medium-, and long-term goals, ongoing collaboration with physicians is essential. Physicians are comfortable providing pharmacological management and whatever follow-up contacts they believe are appropriate. Issues around employment can be an intermittent or an ongoing problem, one that may come and go as promotions or job changes occur. The practitioner may need to work with the patient's employer to establish appropriate accommodations at the job site. Or, if employers are uncooperative, the practitioner may participate in administrative hearings or provide court testimony for issues involving "reasonable accommodations" as mandated by federal law such as the Americans for Disabilities Act of 1990.

Working with adults with ADHD is enormously gratifying and rewarding. They seek help to function better, and they are appreciative of the efforts made on their behalf. The first few evaluations may seem tedious, difficult, and perhaps frustrating. However, this will pass as the practitioner adapts his or her psychological skills, training, and treatment interventions to the adult ADHD population. I am confident my fellow clinicians will enjoy working with them. Once a clinician's credentials in adult ADHD treatment are known, one can generally anticipate a significant increase in his or her referral base as word of mouth spreads in the community about "somebody who might know what's wrong with me and knows how to help me."

Appendix:
Adult ADHD Resources

Annotated Bibliography

The following is not intended to be an exhaustive list, as ADHD in adulthood is an expanding area. Listed are books dealing with day-to-day living and self-help strategies for adults with ADHD and also references for professionals working in the ADHD field.

PUBLICATIONS FOR ADULTS WITH ADHD

Children and Adults with Attention Deficit Disorder. (1997). *ADD and adults: Strategies for success from CHADD*. Plantation, FL: Author.

>   This paperback is a compilation of short articles on ADHD in adults published by CHADD and from *CHADDerBOX* and *ATTENTION!* Recent articles cover issues on the job, employment, and interpersonal relationships.

Hallowell, E. M., & Ratey, J. J. (1995). *Driven to distraction: Recognizing and coping with attention deficit disorder from childhood through adulthood*. New York: Simon & Schuster.

>   Probably the biggest "best seller" in the area of ADHD, this book tracks the disorder from childhood to adulthood. This book, which has some interesting chapters on treatment, is the one that most adults coming into my practice mention.

Hallowell, E. M., & Ratey, J. J. (1996). *Answers to distraction*. New York: Bantam Books.

>   The authors expand on their earlier book with an increased focus on management and interventions.

Halverstadt, J. S. (1988). *ADD & romance: Finding fulfillment in love, sex, & relationships*. Dallas, TX: Taylor Publishing.

A book dealing with the trials and tribulations of ADHD adults in love. Problems with communication, intimacy, and sharing (among others) are discussed and coping strategies are described.

Hartmann, T. (1993). *Attention deficit disorder: A different perception*. Grass Valley, CA: Underwood Books.

The author takes a different view of attention deficits, seeing them as a natural, evolving, adaptive trait and viewing individuals as either "hunters" or "farmers." The book includes some discussion of behavioral intervention and strategies.

Jackson, M. T. (1997). *The adult attention deficit disorders intervention manual*. Columbia, MO: Hawthorne Educational Services.

This good, simple intervention manual states an ADHD problem, such as being disorganized with possessions at home or work, and then lists about 50 strategies or behaviors to resolve the problem.

Kelly, K., & Ramundo, P. (1995). *You mean I'm not lazy, stupid, or crazy?!: A Self-help book for adults with attention deficit disorder*. New York: Scribner.

This is one of my favorite books to recommend to adults with ADHD. The authors both have ADHD, and they recognize the need for short paragraphs, short chapters, and cartoon breaks. Although the book has information on diagnosis and pharmacological management, its power is in the behaviorally based strategies and the commonsense approach. This is one of the best self-help books available.

Latham, P. S., & Latham, P. H. (1992). *Learning disabilities and the law*. Washington, DC: JKL Communications.

The authors address two general classes of rights—civil and educational/disability—and survey laws and legal remedies. Written in lay terms, the book is helpful for adults seeking workplace accommodations under the Americans with Disabilities Act of 1990.

Nadeau, K. G. (1996). *Adventures in fast forward: Life, love, and work for the ADD adult*. New York: Brunner/Mazel.

In this book the author spends considerable time on diagnosis, symptoms, and treatment options. The sections on intervention are well done, and readers will certainly find strategies that they had not considered before. This book, the first general book on ADHD to deal specifically with gender, is high on my list of recommended reading for patients.

Nadeau, K. G. (1997). *ADD in the workplace: Choices, changes, and challenges*. New York: Brunner/Mazel.

As the title suggests, the book focuses on workplace and career issues. Included are discussions about the kinds of suitable and antithetical employment for adults with ADHD.

Novotni, M. (1999). *What does everybody else know that I don't? Social skills help for adults with attention deficit hyperactivity disorders.* Plantation, FL: Specialty Press.

> A very good read for ADHD individuals who make social errors and have problems with social skills. A self-help book.

Quinn, P. O. (1994). *ADD and the college student: A guide for high school and college students with attention deficit disorder.* Washington, DC: Magination Press.

> This book may be helpful for late teens and college students with attention deficits. It provides recommendations on compensations, admissions, and scholastic aptitude tests.

Solden, S. (1995). *Women with attention deficit disorders: Embracing disorganization at home and in the workplace.* Grass Valley, CA: Underwood Books.

> This is the only book in print that deals exclusively with women with attention deficits and their impact on growth and development, work, and role as primary caregivers. I recommend this book to each newly diagnosed woman with ADHD, as it encourages her to redefine and restructure her life. It is a good read.

Weiss, L. (1998). *Attention deficit disorder in adults: Practical help and understanding* (3rd ed.). Dallas, TX: Taylor.

> This book is also high on my recommend list because it enables spouses or significant others of adults with ADHD to understand more about the disorder, recognizing that ADHD symptoms are the explanation (and not the excuse) for many of the problems in the relationship. In addition, the book tries to resolve those problems by offering strategies that the non-ADHD partner can use.

PUBLICATIONS FOR PROFESSIONALS

Barkley, R. A. (1998). *Attention-deficit/hyperactivity disorder: A handbook for diagnosis and treatment* (2nd ed.). New York: Guilford Press.

> This book is an excellent resource, as it addresses both theoretical and practical approaches to the understanding of ADHD through the life span. This is a rigorously researched and well-documented volume, and it has a solid chapter on ADD in adulthood.

Bhandary, A. N., Fernandez, F., Gregory, R. J., Tucker, P., & Masand, P. (1997). Pharmacotherapy in adults with ADHD. *Psychiatric Annals, 27,* 545–555.

> This is a good article on the use of various pharmacological agents (however, Adderall is not included, simply because it had not been on the market long enough to be researched and reported).

Dulcan, M. K., & Benson, R. S. (1997). Summary of the practice parameters for the assessment and treatment of children, adolescents, and adults with ADHD. *Journal of the American Academy of Child and Adolescent Psychiatry, 36*, 1311–1316.

This article provides a general overview of the field and discusses effective and ineffective treatments.

Elia, J., Ambrosini, P. J., & Rapoport, J. L. (1999). Drug therapy: Treatment of attention-deficit-hyperactivity disorder. *New England Journal of Medicine, 340*, 780–788.

This article is an excellent overview of ADHD, including prevalence, genetics, course, and treatments.

Hunt, R. D. (1997). Nosology, neurobiology and clinical patterns of ADHD in adults. *Psychiatric Annals, 27*, 572–580.

This is a good discussion of biology and brain function in ADHD.

Jackson, M. T. (1997). *The attention deficit disorders intervention manual.* New York: Hawthorne Educational Services.

The author has operationalized 57 problems frequently seen in adults with ADHD. For each, multiple intervention strategies are recommended. This book is a good guide to developing, at least initially, behavioral interventions.

Latham, P., & Latham, P. H. (1992). *Attention deficit disorder and the law.* Washington, DC: JKL Communications.

The two authors are attorneys who have had extensive experience in ADHD. This excellent book discusses federal laws and mandates, including the Rehabilitation Act of 1973, with particular emphasis on Section 504; the newly reauthorized Individuals with Disabilities Education Act; and the Americans for Disabilities Act of 1990.

Nadeau, K. G. (1996). *ADD in the workplace: Choices, changes, and challenges.* New York: Brunner/Mazel.

This is a great resource for workplace issues and strategies.

Wender, P. H. (1995). *Attention-deficit/hyperactivity disorder in adults.* New York: Oxford University Press.

This author, who has a long history in writing about this disorder, presents a straightforward and pragmatic approach to the biological and psychological components of ADHD. This book is well researched, and the description of the biological components of ADHD is perhaps the best written.

Wilens, T. E., Biederman, J., & Spencer, T. J. (1998). Pharmacotherapy of attention deficit hyperactivity disorder in adults. *Disease Management, 9*, 347–356.

A more recent article on medication management in adults, it is helpful in understanding the how and why of the classes of medication.

National Organizations and Support Groups

ADDO Foundation

Station R, Box 223, Toronto, Ontario M46 2S9 Canada
416-813-6858
http://www.addofoundation.org/
This organization provides ADD information, offers adult and parent support groups, and offers "cyber mentoring."

ADDult Information Exchange Network

Box 1991, Ann Arbor, MI 48106
734-426-1659
http://www.addien.org/
This organization, which serves as a clearinghouse, provides helpful information for adults with ADHD and also conferences for professionals.

Attention Deficit Information Network (AD-IN)

475 Hillside Avenue, Needham, MA 02194
617-455-9895
AD-IN provides information about regional meetings and current research. It also offers practical ideas regarding practical problems faced by adults with attention deficits. The organization has chapters in Massachusetts, Ohio, New Hampshire, New Jersey, South Carolina, and West Virginia.

Children and Adults with Attention Deficit Disorder (CHADD)

8181 Professional Place, Suite 201, Landover, MD 20785
1-800-233-4050 or 301-306-7070
http://www.chadd.org/
CHADD is the largest organization of its kind, with over 500 chapters in the United States and Canada. As a former member of the professional board, I know firsthand the quality of the work that they do. Membership in CHADD includes receiving *CHADDerBOX*, its newsletter, and *ATTENTION!*, a quarterly magazine. A call to the toll-free number will provide the closest CHADD chapter, as will a visit to the Web site. The Web site also has regular updates on diagnosis, treatment, educational, and other relevant issues.

National Attention Deficit Disorder Association (NADDA)

1788 Second Street, Suite 200, Highland Park, IL 60035
1-800-487-2332
http://www.add.org/
NADDA is a national group providing educational literature and assistance and also support groups to adults with ADHD.

Newsletters/Magazines

ADD ONS
A bimonthly "paper support group" for those living with ADHD.
P.O. Box 675, Frankfort, IL 60423
815-334-1128

ADDult News
A quarterly newsletter on ADD.
ADDult Support Network, c/o Mary Jane Johnson, 2620 Ivy Place, Toledo, OH 43613

ADDitude
An excellent print and internet magazine for current information on ADHD in adulthood; it appears to be updated regularly.
http://www.additudemag.com/

ADDvance
A bimonthly magazine for women with ADD.
Advantage Books
1001 Spring Street, Suite 118, Silver Spring, MD 20910
1-888-238-8588
http://www.addvance.com/

ATTENTION!
A quarterly magazine that comes as a benefit of membership in CHADD (see above).

CHADDerBOX
A monthly magazine that comes as a benefit of membership in CHADD (see above).

FOCUS
A quarterly magazine that comes as a benefit of membership in CHADD (see above).

Resource Material

ADD WareHouse
300 Northwest 70th Avenue, Suite 102, Plantation, FL 33317
1-800-233-9273 or 954-792-8100
http://www.addwarehouse.com/
This free catalog, which I regularly show to patients, contains the most extensive list of books, training programs, videos, computerized tests of attention, and so forth for purchase by professionals and people with ADHD.

Major Listservs

America OnLine
Use e-mail to contact the following hosts: susans29@aol.com, debette@ aol.com, annie12345@aol.com, maryd@aol.com, jimams@aol.com, and ericnjb@aol.com. Or as these sites may change, use Go ADD.

Compuserv
Get to GO ADD or email 70006.101@cv.com

Prodigy
On this server, look under medical support, and then look for the attention deficit disorder topic.

Miscellaneous

Attention Deficit Disorder Information Packet
NIH Neurological Institute, P.O. Box 5801, Bethesda, MD 20824
1-800-352-9424
http://www.nimh.nih.gov/publicat/adhd.cfm/
This is a packet of information based on NIH studies regarding ADHD. This site, which is updated regularly, also has an interesting color photograph of positron emitting tomography showing the differences in neurochemical firing in an ADHD and a non-ADHD cerebral cortex.

Health-Center.com
http://www.health-center.com/
A general site for information about ADHD, its diagnosis, and treatment.

Learning Disabilities Association of America
4156 Library Road, Pittsburgh, PA 15234
412-341-8077
This is a post–high school clearinghouse of information for individuals with disabilities.

Rebus Institute
198 Taylor Boulevard, Suite 201, Millbrae, CA 94030
The organization deals with the Americans with Disabilities Act and its impact on the workplace.

Note. All information is accurate as of April 2000.

Index

About the Author

Robert J. Resnick, PhD, FAClinP, is a health/clinical psychologist and recently "retired" as a professor of psychiatry and pediatrics and chair of the Division of Clinical Psychology at Virginia Commonwealth University (VCU). In 1984 he created and directed an Attention Deficit Disorders Clinic at VCU. He is now a professor of psychology at Randolph-Macon College in Ashland, Virginia, and maintains a specialty practice in attention deficit hyperactivity disorders through the life span.

Dr. Resnick has received many awards for his contributions to professional practice, including the American Psychological Association (APA) Board of Professional Affairs Award for Contributions to Professional Practice, the APA Division 12 (clinical psychology) Award for Contributions to Professional Practice, the Lee Salk Award from the Society of Pediatric Psychology, and the Outstanding Civilian Service Medal from the U.S. Department of the Army. He is a diplomate in clinical psychology and a distinguished practitioner in the National Academy of Practice. He serves on the editorial boards of several journals and has presented and published widely on attention deficits both through the life span and in relation to health care policy.

Dr. Resnick was president of the APA from 1995 to 1996 and is a past-president of the APA's Division 42 (independent practice). His interest in attention deficit disorders and their impact on individuals and their families began 25 years ago. Dr. Resnick has been married to his wife, Fran, for 36 years, and has one son, Steven, and two daughters, Danielle and Jolene.